AF269600

Praise for *Leveling Up*

Leveling up: Adoptive Parents and the Adult Adoptee is a long overdue contribution to the field of Child Welfare. It reminds us that adopted individuals do not remain babies or children and that their parents' goal is for them to emancipate and become functioning adults in their community as well as staying connected to the families from which they launched. This task is made more complex by the fact of adoption, which this book explores thoroughly, and also offers tools by which parents and their young adults can accomplish this developmental stage. The two authors use their years of professional experience and their life as adoptive parents to offer the readers a balanced and rich perspective.

Sharon Kaplan Roszia M.S.
*Seven Core Issues in Adoption and Permanency: A Comprehensive Guide to Promoting Understanding and Healing in Adoption, Foster Care, Kinship Families and Third-Party Reproductio*n. Roszia and Maxon. Jessica Kingsley Press, 000

Advanced Praise for *Leveling Up!* I embrace the belief that the act of adoption is beautiful and at the heart of God as reflected in His word. I recognize that God never promised adoptive parenting or that the adoptee journey would be easy! Quite often adoptive parenting requires being counterintuitive: what the parent *thinks* is an appropriate response may actually be words that weaken the bond between parent and child. As seasoned adoptive mothers and professionals, Elaine and Christina offer practical advice sprinkled with humor and real-life, raw examples. Their combined lived experiences have depth and shed light on the complexities of the journey for both parents and adoptees alike. I commend *Leveling Up* to everyone who has invested in adoption, be it as an adoptee, an adoptive parent, a professional in the field, pastors & counselors who serve the adoption & foster care community and those who are curious and want to learn more.

Lisa M. Troncale, LSW and Adoptive Mother
Truman Counseling Services

What a much-needed book for the adoption community! This age and stage is so underrepresented in all the resources.
Melissa Corkum, adoptee and co-founder, The Adoption Connection

Leveling Up is an honest, practical, and hope-filled book that was as much eye-opening as it was heart calming about a topic many feel resigned to navigate alone. The transparent guidance on navigating actual challenges that will help shepherd families we serve. This age demographic is often overlooked and it was refreshingly truthful to hear from Elaine and Christiana about the journey they are on with their kids, who become adults, but remain precious children to God and their parents. If you are tired, confused, scared, or simply feeling like you are floating through life amidst the choppy waters of adoption – regardless of whether you are ap parent, teen, adult, or caseworker, this book is for you. With down to earth stories, relevant topics, and uber-practical advice for us, Elaine and Christina model a right posture to love like Jesus yearns for us to love, come what may.
Ryan Keith, Advocate for vulnerable families for 20 years
Community Engagement Pastor, West Shore Free Church

From their personal stories to the take-aways for both caretakers and adoptee, this book is definitely a helpful tool to read and reread as we navigate walking through life with our kids. Thank you, Elaine and Christina, for reminding us that "Love is a feeling, but it is more often a choice" and how important it is that "we choose to love a person in their unloveliness", just like Christ does with us.
Emily Schmidt
Founder & Executive Director, The Cracked Pot Coffee Shop

As an adult adoptee, I found this book to be a great resource. Elaine and Christina approached this project from an honest and reflective space, as they dove deep into the numerous struggles that show up while parenting and preparing adult adoptees. They do extremely well in presenting specific examples, through their personal reflections, as well as suggesting practical tips in moving forward. I see people striving to know exactly how to support adult adoptees (seeking a manual of sorts) but I think people need to understand the trauma that stirs up the emotional needs of the adoptee - and this book does BOTH!
I pondered my own journey as I considered ways in which I can improve in my own interpersonal relationships. While reading, I felt challenged while

also feeling deeply understood. To experience and hold both feelings can be rare, which is why I believe this book could be used as a powerful tool not just for adoptive parents but also for adult adoptees.
Sara R. Odicio, LSW - Founder of CORE of Adoption, LLC

Leveling Up is a much-needed adoptive parenting book that fills a gap in adoption resources. While much has been written on the topic of raising kids who have experienced trauma, very little has been written on parenting young adult children who are in the midst of transitioning into independent living. Authors Christina Reese and Elaine Shenk have both walked parenting journeys with their own adopted children and have valuable insights and experiences to share from their personal experiences. Having worked with adoptive parents for many years, I have witnessed firsthand how some of the most challenging years for adoptive parent are the 'twenties' as adoptees are navigating independence. Leveling Up deals directly with parenting these difficult years and parents will find numerous practical ideas and strategies. Each chapter concludes with thoughtful insights directed to parents, professionals, and adult adoptees as well. Through this book you will gain practical information for how to set healthy boundaries, have challenging conversations and remain grounded in faith through difficult seasons of parenting. By reading Leveling Up you will be encouraged that you are not alone on the adoptive parenting journey and those who have gone before you are cheering you on!
Karen Springs, author of Adoption Through the Rearview Mirror: Learning from Stories of Heartache and Hope

High praise for Leveling Up! This unique book will prove invaluable to therapists, teachers, social workers and of course, adoptive parents and adoptees themselves. As a therapist and an adoptee myself, this book resonated deeply on many levels. I believe it will help normalize and validate the experiences of parents and their kids at various stages of development. It is a long-overdue resource with practical steps for families that will undoubtedly help ease the stress on families navigating unique and uncharted waters that come with adoptive relationships. Well done!
Gina Birkemeier, MAC, LPC, Author of Generations Deep: Unmasking Inherited Dysfunction and Trauma to Rewrite Our Stories Through Faith and Therapy

Leveling Up

ADOPTIVE PARENTS
AND THE ADULT ADOPTEE

Christina Reese, PhD LCPC
Elaine Shenk, MS

CrossLink Publishing
RAPID CITY, SD

Reese and Shenk/CrossLink Publishing
1601 Mt Rushmore Rd. Ste 3288
Rapid City, SD 57701
www.CrossLinkPublishing.com

Ordering Information:
Quantity sales. Special discounts are available on quantity purchases by corporations, associations, and others. For details, contact the "Special Sales Department" at the address above.

Leveling Up/ Christina Reese, PhD LCPC
and Elaine Shenk, MS. —1st ed.

ISBN 978-1-63357-424-3
Library of Congress Control Number: 2022931844

Christina: *To my husband, who is my rock. To my daughter, who is in my heart forever. And to my Jesus, who holds me up on the days I come to the end of myself.*

Elaine: *To my mother, who showed me how to love your children fiercely. To my husband, for being my partner through it all. To my children, I love you forever. And to Jesus, who is my Source of Hope.*

Contents

Foreword

Having worked in the field of adoption for many years, I have met families who fiercely insist that an adoptive family is just like any other family and others who insist, just as fiercely, that there are big differences. Both are true. Families formed by adoption seek to build connection and develop deep and abiding love just like any other family. They navigate relationships and challenges, both within the family and with those outside of its boundaries. But there are also often other layers of challenges for the family formed by adoption. A truism of adoption is that every adoption is born of loss, for children, birth families and adoptive families. That place of loss is also the birthplace of many of the challenges adoptive families face.

Another truism is that every adoption journey is as unique as the children and adults who are involved. Each brings their own personality and formative experiences as well as differing reasons that necessitated adoption in the first place. No two journeys are the same or two families just alike. Yet every journey faces many of the same challenges as well. It can be a lonely journey for the parent (or teen) who feels that their experiences are unlike those of anyone else, or who may be afraid that no one will understand the complex and sometimes competing feelings that they have. Support is vital and that support can come in many forms, listening and non-judgmental friends or family, official or spontaneous support groups, online communities, or books that communicate 'you are not alone!'

As we know, parenting does not magically end when a child turns eighteen and has legal rights and responsibilities. In those late teen years, parents and their teens often find themselves navigating a new relationship, needing to support while trying to find that sometimes elusive balance of help and personal responsibility. It can be a minefield for any parent but for the parent through adoption, the landscape can be particularly fraught with those landmines.

Adoptive mothers and adoption practitioners Elaine Shenk and Christina Reese have collaborated on a book that communicates 'you are not alone in this!' They have come together with their array of both personal and professional experiences to offer both help and hope in an area where they have felt a significant lack of resources for other families formed by adoption. Their deep love and desire to connect with their children who came to them through adoption is so apparent! To quote the deeply loved and respected late Dr. Karyn Purvis, these are children who have come from 'hard places' and carry extra 'baggage' in their journey to love and trust. And Elaine and Christina, with Dr. Purvis' work deeply ingrained into their approach, have taken their experiences, including lessons learned, and shared them openly so that others may both benefit and possibly not feel so alone in the struggle.

While they write openly and honestly about their journeys, these are their journeys and reflect the culmination of experiences that each brought to parenting. Their journey may not be exactly the same as the readers journey, but they share wisdom and love in a way that there are lessons for any reader. Elaine and Christina have been open and vulnerable in their sharing, what they've learned and what they maybe wish had gone differently.

There is great value in hearing someone else's experiences, what wisdom was gained. They are generous in sharing their tips and ideas, made richer and fuller by their professional practices. Their openness offers support to the parent or young adult who may be feeling very alone in the struggle. Reading that someone else has had a similar struggle and hearing how they handled and survived it can be so very valuable. The tips at the end of each chapter make this a very useable resource to return whenever needed for both parent and young adult

Parenting, or the need for parents, does not end at the age of eighteen, but changes and evolves over time. Elaine and Christina have provided a guide for anyone seeking to navigate the unfamiliar territory of young adulthood, and to do it without losing sight of, as Dr. Purvis would say, the preciousness of each of our children.

May we always be willing to openly share our journey in a way that can smooth the path, even just a little, for the next traveler.

—Kris Faasse, LMSW, ACSW

Preface

On this journey of parenting our adopted children, we have reached a new chapter. Our children are now young adults. In our experience, there seems to be an absence of guidance, of helpful literature or information, and a shortage of encouraging voices who have gone before. Perhaps you are going around this bend with us and are also finding the terrain unfamiliar or particularly bumpy. Even the young adult adoptees we work with are looking for others with whom to process their adoption journeys so they can develop healthy, intimate attachments with partners and children. So, as we collaborated professionally and shared personally, we thought we would share what we have learned!

The challenge of parenting children through the ages of eighteen to twenty-five is that they want to make their own choices. Yet, as their brains continue to grow and develop, they are not helping them to make consistently good choices. These young adults need parents to consult, with whom they can problem-solve and to whom they can turn for support. Adopted children in this age group also have a developmentally unfinished brain. The adoption itself then further complicates this developmental stage. The adoptee has experienced relational trauma and, as a result, has a harder time trusting their parents. When adopted children do not trust their parents, they do not return to them for support, problem-solving, or consultation. The result is that they feel alone in the world, trying to prove they do not need anyone and can manage themselves.

The hard part for wise parents is knowing that children are not ready to do life all by themselves. These parents desire to be the support that parents are meant to be, but how? How to stay connected to their kids when those kids are trying so hard to pull away? How can these kids be launched successfully? How do parents offer consultation, support, and problem-solving without pushing their kids away?

Many can benefit from this book, beginning with professionals working in the field of adoption and foster care, who can glean insight into training parents for the lifelong commitment they are making to a child. This book can give them tools and understanding for supporting children and families in the latter years and for helping families to not give up hope. Adult adoptees can also use this book to encourage discussion with their parents. Perhaps you haven't been able to find the words to tell your mom and dad what you need, but as you read this book together, you can come to a clearer understanding of the process of attaching and letting go. Finally, adoptive and foster parents can learn ways to reframe their child's "launch" into adulthood and provide supports to make it a positive and relationship-building experience for all involved.

We are walking down this road with you. We may be in front of, behind, or beside you. We have successes and failures to share. We have done research and formed community-based support networks for ourselves and our kids. We hope that by sharing our journeys, we can help you on yours.

I (Elaine) have four children, each of whom joined our family through adoption. The first three were domestic infant adoptions and the last one was a foster care adoptive placement. Each of the children have their own stories of how they got here and of what adoption has been like for them. The stories I share in this book are my stories of being their mom. I've asked their permission to write about them and they've agreed. I've also given them the opportunity to have a first glance at what has been shared. Some of the stories involve a mixture of the kids, so even if you know us, you may not be sure which child I'm talking about. Being the mother of these children has been the greatest gift I could ever have. They've brought me so much joy, love, and beauty. My heart overflows. Being their mom has also broken, humbled, polished, and made me stronger and more empathetic. I keep going because adoption is a lifelong journey.

I have been working in the social services field for over a decade, walking beside many other families in all phases of adoption. I especially love training families, whether through pre-adoptive classes as they are preparing to become an adoptive family, or post adoptive training, working with families who have been built through adoption. My joy is sitting in parent consultations and helping them find hope as they reframe what is going on in their homes. Often, looking at behaviors through a different lens changes their perspective. Parents begin to understand the need behind the behaviors and can respond instead of react. I often hear, "If I can just get her to age eighteen and send her to college, we are good to go!" The clock is ticking toward the magical cut-off date, and parents are realizing "eighteen years old" might not be so magical! I sit with them and agree, "It's hard." It's hard to be the parents of adult children. It's hard to be the parent of an adult adoptee. I let them know it is possible that when we as parents quit being parents when our children reach a certain age, we destroy the possibility of our children finding healing. This is the same healing we have wanted them to have all along. All because they didn't find it before the age of eighteen.

So, we hold onto hope.

> I remain confident of this; I will see the goodness of the Lord in the land of the living. Wait for the Lord; be strong and take heart and wait for the Lord. (Psalm 27:13–14 NIV)

This was one of my favorite verses while going through dark times with my family. My faith was very important to me; I needed something solid and unshakeable when everything around me was shifting. So, I held onto this. What I found was, I was also holding onto hope for my children, who couldn't hold onto it for themselves.

I (Christina) knew I was going to adopt at the age of fourteen. I had spent the summer working at an orphanage in a third world country and fell in love. I loved the country, the children, and the culture. Over the next ten years I worked in orphanages four times, in two countries. Each time I felt my heart's desire to adopt confirmed. I began "nesting." I bought a house, finished my college degrees, and began working as a mental health therapist. I have now been working with children and families for over twenty years, specializing in trauma and attachment. I have written books and spoken around the world about attachment, trauma, and children. Working with adoptive families—helping them to become a family—is my favorite work.

When I adopted my sweet girl from the country I fell in love with, she was fourteen and came home as a child from a "hard place." We both had to work through learning to become a family. We are still on that journey today.

We (Elaine and Christina) are writing this book together because Elaine is a few years ahead of Christina's parenting journey and is beginning to come out on the other side. We've learned some things from our children and experiences, both personally and professionally. The most important thing we have learned is this: Parents don't get done being parents. Our job is to keep walking beside our children, supporting them, encouraging them, and showing up. It doesn't mean taking over, keeping them down, or holding them back. It is their life. They will make mistakes and fail, and so will we. But we keep walking beside them.

This book is divided into sections. Perhaps not all of them are applicable to you. It is fine to jump around between chapters. You can also read straight through, gleaning the best parts for your situation. At the end of each chapter are "takeaways" for parents, professionals, and adult adoptees. None of this is "one size fits all" but it is a great starting place for asking good questions and getting the support you need as the forever family you are!

CHAPTER 1

Loving a Child Who Has Experienced Trauma

When a child is adopted, the parents may not have been aware that the child was going to be bringing trauma into their house. The parents were probably aware their child might be bringing thoughts and feelings about their biological parents such as curiosity or a desire to search for them later. They may have even been aware there could be developmental delays due to possible substance abuse during the pregnancy. Parents may have known that their child had a physical or intellectual disability, and been prepared for the many therapies and doctors' appointments. Yet many adoptive parents are not aware of the trauma.

I (Elaine) was diagnosed with polycystic ovary syndrome (PCOS) in my teens. It was a new diagnosis at that time, and I was told I would probably have trouble getting pregnant. I took that prediction to heart and announced to my husband, early in our relationship, "If you want to have a child that looks like you or aren't okay with adopting, you might want to bail out now!" He didn't jump ship, but I'm sure there has been more than one occasion in over thirty years of marriage when he wondered if he should have asked more questions up front!

I (Christina) adopted internationally as a single woman and married my best friend eighteen months later. To say our house was full of transition for years is an understatement! To say our family is still working on becoming a family is accurate. My husband is my rock on the hard days and helps me to celebrate the good ones.

In both of our situations, we knew we wanted to adopt and went into it with our eyes wide open. There were days we were not sure we would make it, days we felt we had reached the end of ourselves. These were the days when we had to lean heavily into the arms of Jesus, trusting that He does not make mistakes. He finishes the good work He begins. He does not leave us alone. The reason we had these overwhelming emotions of hopelessness and of wondering if we would make it was because of the trauma our children had gone through to join our families.

In the Beginning . . .
What is trauma? Medical events and life-threatening illnesses, community and family violence, and natural disasters are understood to be traumatic. When it is said a foster or adopted child has "experienced trauma," what does that mean? With increasing research, there is a greater understanding that even adopted children who have joined families from birth have experienced trauma. This is trauma's common thread: Feelings of safety and security have been taken away. This sense of loss of safety and security becomes the scaffolding for the rest of the child's development.

Every adopted child has specifically experienced attachment or relationship trauma, which impacts their ability to feel safe and secure, especially in relationships. Many adoptive parents, especially those who have adopted infants, cannot believe this would be so. "But our baby came to us at birth!" "We were in the Labor and Delivery Room with her birth mother!" "His joining

our family was the happiest day of our lives!" What is often for-
gotten is that relationship building begins before birth.

Attachment begins in utero when the baby begins hearing at
eighteen weeks of development. The baby listens, for four-and-
a-half months before birth, all day, every day, to their biological
mother's heartbeat. This becomes their first safe place, secure
base, and comfort zone. When a baby is born, they leave a place
that is dark, quiet, and warm to move into an environment that
is cold, bright, and loud, an experience known as sensory over-
stimulation. At birth, a baby is also separated from the biological
mother's heartbeat, adding to the child's distress.

When experiencing this distress, the baby will cry, using his
voice to express his need for comfort and connection. A newborn baby is often placed on the mother's chest, even before the
umbilical cord is severed. Most babies calm because they have returned to their comfort zone and safe place by hearing Mother's
heartbeat again. For the adopted child, they are separated from
this heartbeat, safe place, and comfort zone, never to return. A
baby will cry for their biological mother's heartbeat. When not
re-unified with their primary attachment figure, they can lose
trust in attachment-based relationships. When that infant is separated from their biological parent, even if it is to their excited,
loving, adoptive parents' arms, they are experiencing their first
attachment trauma.

I (Elaine) didn't know this when we brought our oldest one
home at twenty-five days old. Not much was known then about
adoption-related trauma. I wanted to be a good mom, but we
were told "good babies" slept in their own crib down the hall, in
their nursery, through the night by themselves. My baby cried
and cried! Oh, what I would give to be able to go back there and
hold her through the night to let her know she wasn't going to
lose me, that I would be her safe place!

While a baby will not have a visual memory of this loss and
grief, she will have a sense memory of loss and distrust. The five

senses, which are active at birth (and some before birth), are recording information about the environment, presenting it to the brain for categorization. Information gets recorded into the brain in the form of grooves, or neural pathways. A child, using sensory memory, will remember a sound, a smell, or a touch that will evoke a feeling or sensation. When it is based in trauma—that is, a loss of safety and security—this feeling often moves the child to anxiety, causing the release of cortisol and adrenaline.

For the child who has been in foster or orphanage care, which means multiple homes or caregivers, each change is an additional attachment trauma. It is a rupture that creates a barrier in the child's ability to trust in the security of relationships. This influences all relationships moving forward unless healing is brought to the child's ability to trust in vulnerability. They can have difficulty in connecting to other parent figures, dating and marriage relationships, friendships, and even their relationships with their own children in years to come. Their template for relationship building is based in trauma, not in healthy relationship skills like trust, vulnerability, and attunement (meeting each other's needs mutually).

In addition to the trauma that happens when children are separated from their biological parents, cases of abuse and neglect compound a child's trauma: Harm has occurred within a relationship meant for protection and security. For the child who has experienced abuse, each incident of abuse has been recorded by their senses. Once a neural pathway is created by the first experience, each additional abusive incident is recorded into the same pathway. This causes further deepening of and investment in that groove until it is the child's default, or "belief system." A belief system about adults is created from experiences of abuse, especially when there is no other context with which to compare them. This belief system then changes the child's ability to feel safe with other adults and to follow their directions. Typically, they do not follow the directions of those with whom they do not feel safe. If a child has had the experience that adults (or prior caregivers) aren't safe people, then the child's belief system generalizes that *all adults are not safe people.*

When a child's needs are not met, even as early as a few hours old, that child will use his voice to alert the adults that he has a need. Needs include food, shelter, clothing, safety, and love. He will cry, but when his cries go unanswered due to neglect, he will stop using his voice to get his needs met and will begin using his behaviors to meet his own needs independently.

I (Christina) saw this when I worked in orphanages for very young children. I would walk into a room with twenty cribs lining the walls. There was a baby in each crib. They were all wide awake and it was silent. That silence was the most horrific sound I have ever heard. I would make sure that when I went into one of those rooms, I had enough time to hold each baby. Once they realized someone was picking up and holding babies, they all pulled up and quietly waited their turn, watching intently. I often think about those babies, look at their pictures, and wonder where they are now. Do their parents know and understand that their twenty-three-year-old child was not held as a baby, and how that has impacted them? Is that child able to trust in the security of relationships and use their words to express their needs in relationships?

In the first year of life, a child's only social developmental goal is to learn how to trust. He uses his voice to let others know his needs, learning to trust that when those needs are met, they will continue to be met moving forward. When a healthy parent responds to each cry and meets each need, a baby learns to trust that his voice is important, that he is valued and precious, and that someone is listening. Someone wants to meet his needs and is able to do so. This is the beginning of healthy self-esteem. When a child does not learn to trust at this developmentally appropriate time, it will be more difficult to develop this foundational relationship skill later in life. If his voice is not validated and responded to, he stops using it. This creates barriers to encouraging him to use his voice in the future. He will have a hard time believing that someone is listening and cares, that he does not need to use behaviors to have his needs met. In fact, each time he maladaptively uses his behaviors to meet his own needs, and it is effective, it is reinforced in his brain, in a neural pathway, that this is the most effective way to have his needs met. It will become his default, his belief system, about having needs met. Belief systems are challenging to change because they are deeply reinforced; they are not only thoughts and feelings that we are trying to change, but foundational building blocks that a child uses to understand the world around them.

When a child's needs are not met, their ability to trust adults to take care of them is impacted. When any needs are not fulfilled for a child, they will attempt to meet those needs by themselves. *Needs* are set apart from *wants* in their necessity for survival. A need must be met. One will search and strive to fill the void with anything that will suffice. When a child is hungry, he will beg, borrow, and steal to secure food because he needs it to survive. The need for love is seen in a child seeking attention and connection. If this need is not met for the child, they will not stop seeking it, even if inappropriately, until the need is met. When we ignore attention-seeking behaviors, we are ignoring a need. Ignoring will not extinguish the behavior like we hope. Instead, it will increase the child's urgency to have the need met, often increasing the severity of the behaviors.

The Anxiety Connection
When a person doesn't feel safe, their natural reaction is to experience anxiety. This natural reaction is the "survival brain" trying to keep them alive and restore safety and stability. The survival brain is the limbic system, the lower portion of the brain which deals with emotions and memory. It is responsible for preserving life. This part of the brain is where survival skills and defense

mechanisms live. Digestion, respiration, and other life-sustaining functions are controlled by this part of the brain. One of the ways our survival brain keeps us safe is by activating the alert system that prepares the body for self-preservation.

When we don't feel safe and the alert system is activated, it sends a message to the adrenal gland to release the hormone adrenaline. It also sends a message to the pituitary gland to release another stress hormone, cortisol. Cortisol can cause our brain to feel "fuzzy," making it difficult to remember tasks and increasing the challenge to have clear, logical thinking. Sound decision-making can become difficult. Adrenaline causes the heart to beat faster, which raises our blood pressure, causing us to feel hot and our face to flush. It causes our lungs to constrict such that we may have trouble breathing and our muscles may tighten. This can result in head- and stomachaches, both of which are common anxiety symptoms. Adrenaline makes us need to move or causes us to feel jittery.

For the child who has experienced trauma, their alert system is often overactive due to its frequent use in protecting the child. Their bodies flood with adrenaline and cortisol, which fuel the anxiety reactions of fight, flight, and freeze. A child's "fight mode" looks like verbal or physical aggression, arguments, and opposition. The child feels unsafe, so their defense mechanisms and survival skills are fully engaged. A child's "flight mode" can manifest in isolating, running away, or doing the opposite of what they are asked to do. When the child feels unsafe, their mind is telling them to leave the area or relationship to restore feelings of safety and security. "Freeze mode" in a child looks like staring into space or "spacing out," not listening, shutting down, or dissociating. This is an effort to escape feeling unsafe, to find a safer place within themselves. The hormones driving these reactions are not based in feelings only, but also in biological changes happening within the body that the child may not be able to manage or control. They are struggling to regulate their bodies and the hormones caused by an anxiety reaction.

Once the child moves into a safe environment, with safe adults, their alert system can remain hypervigilant. It can continue alerting the child to danger even when the child is safe. They are safe but they do not feel safe. The child may be anxious, may not trust parents to be in charge, and may continue to try to control their environment. This overactive alert system results in the behaviors that most adoptive parents are familiar with:

- Aggression
- Elopement
- Hyperactivity
- Opposition
- Defiance
- Refusing to follow directions
- Disrespect
- Distrust
- Fierce independence
- Not allowing the adult to be in control/bossing the adult
- Taking what they need and want/stealing
- Lying
- Explosive emotions
- Anger management challenges

Drinking water and practicing mindfulness are ways in which we use awareness to calm and clear our minds and help reduce the effects of cortisol. Another way to reduce the effect of cortisol is through using good sleep hygiene to get at least eight hours of sleep nightly. Diets rich in proteins and green leafy vegetables can also metabolize the cortisol.

The biological effects of adrenaline (racing heart, rising blood pressure, constricted breathing, tightness in muscles, and head- and stomachaches) are the red flags that parents can teach children to be aware of as their prompt to use coping and calm-ing skills. These physical symptoms can be the cues that a child needs to do some physical activity such as taking a walk, doing a few wall push-ups or jumping jacks, or doing several yoga pos-es. Adrenaline will not dissipate over time but will continue to impact us until we have used or burned it up through physical activity.

In addition, sensory coping skills are especially effective for trauma triggers because the senses record the trauma into grooves in the brain. Those same senses trigger the traumatic memories (when the child smells, hears, or feels a texture that brings back the unsafe feelings based in trauma experiences). We can calm those triggered senses using sensory coping skills. Some of our favorites include:

- Essential oils in diffusers or on cotton balls
- A sound machine where the child can choose to listen to the beach, rain, or white noise
- Tastes, including spicy (cinnamon or spearmint) to lift the mood of a sad child or sweet (bubble gum or butterscotch) to calm an anxious or angry child
- Kinetic sand
- Weighted blankets
- Bins of uncooked beans or rice that children can sift through for toys or objects
- Ice to hold or suck on, or cold water running over the child's hands
- Coloring a mandala or other symmetrical drawing (engag-es both sides of the brain in calming)

But why use one coping skill when you can stack coping skills for maximum benefit! Try these:

- Dancing along to a favorite song on repeat (physical activity while engaging the sense of hearing)
- Chewing gum while playing with kinetic sand (senses of taste, smell, and touch)
- Pulling apart a cotton ball with an essential oil on it (senses of touch and smell)
- Taking a walk while talking out a problem (physical activity with connection in relationship)
- 5-4-3-2-1 (engaging all five senses at the same time)
  - Name five things you can see
  - Name four things you can touch
  - Name three things you can hear
  - Name two things you can smell
  - Name one thing you can taste

Another common survival brain reaction is the need to have control. When we are trying to keep ourselves safe, our natural reaction is to try to control ourselves, our environment, and everyone who comes into our environment. This creates problematic behaviors in children, which look like power struggles and button-pushing to maintain control over the adults that they do not trust as safe people. Others being in control can increase anxiety for children who are not feeling safe. In contrast, when children feel safe and secure, their defense mechanisms and survival skills are disengaged. They are then able to engage in trusting relationships. Sometimes simply sharing power, instead of power-struggling, can calm a child and diffuse an escalation. Parents and other caring adults can do this through giving choices or helping the child to identify areas of their life they do control and exercising healthy control in those areas. Helping the child to identify what they can and cannot control brings a balanced view of control. The things we do not control are those things we need to accept we have no control over. Instead, we use coping and calming skills to regulate. Those things we do control are ones we can problem-solve by creating a plan and working our plan to reduce anxiety responses and increase healthy functioning. A child does control the regulation of their emotions. When parents teach them how to do this, healthy control and feelings of competence are restored.

In addition to these changes in the child's body, trauma also causes large changes in their emotions. Children, when they feel unsafe, have strong feelings of scared, sad, and then angry. Anger is a secondary emotion, coming from feelings of sad and scared that were not resolved. Angry feelings can be based on no one helping the child to feel safe and secure, or not helping them to care for the sad and scared emotions that seemed to engulf them. Strong emotions can easily control or overcome a child, especially if the child does not know how to control those emotions using coping and calming skills or emotion regulation. For the child who has been abused or neglected by biological parents, those parents most likely were not helping the child to calm the feelings that resulted from these traumas. The child is left with strong feelings and no instruction on how to deal with them. The adoptive parent, and those working with the family, must remember that this is happening inside the child's mind and body.

The Impact of Disrupted Development
In the first five years of life, many foundational skills are taught to children by their primary caregiver. Relational, social and emotion regulation skills are not part of our DNA. They are not instinctual. These skills must be taught by someone else. Teaching can come through verbal instruction, but it comes most often through modeling. Relationship skills are taught as the parent develops a relationship with the child from birth. Parents either respond to the child's voice and needs, modeling how to be vulnerable and build trust, or ignore the child's voice and needs, modeling independence and a disconnect that is not healthy or developmentally appropriate. The child will only know the

relationship skills he has been taught, whether appropriate or inappropriate. For children raised in foster care or in orphanages, where their care is being administered by different adults each day, confusion can be created about a parent's role and indiscriminate connections.

Social skills are also taught within these busy developmental years. A child is watching and listening to the way their caregiver interacts with those around them, both within and outside the home. If a parent is kind and respectful to their spouse, the grocery clerk, or other relatives, this is what is normalized for the child as the way to interact with others. In contrast, if the parent treats those around them with disrespect, verbal abuse, and even bullying behaviors, these are what are modeled and normalized for the child as appropriate social skills.

Finally, a caregiver teaches emotion regulation to a child during these years. A child cannot emotionally regulate themselves, but instead co-regulates with the adult who is with them. If a parent is responding to life situations with anxiety, modeling this as an appropriate reaction, the child will begin to respond in the same way. They will have an anxious response to many of life's events. If a parent responds to feelings of anger by throwing objects and hitting others, this is what is modeled for the child as an appropriate way to express emotions. The child will begin to express their anger in the same ways. However, if a parent is emotionally regulated (cool, calm, and collected) when faced with a challenging situation (perhaps even a tantrumming child), the child will be able to find their calm based on their parent's regulation. They will learn to respond to distressing situations with calming and coping skills because that is what their parent has taught them through modeling. Remember, children do not have context. What they experience in childhood becomes their foundation and belief system. This is how healthy or maladaptive relational, social, and emotion-regulation skills develop.

Children whose needs are not met by adults will begin trying to meet their own needs. Some children are convinced that they alone need to take care of themselves. These children rise up in independence, developing self-sufficiency earlier than is age and developmentally appropriate. They no longer trust adults to take care of them—not that they did much before. Often, this child will say things like, "I'll do it myself," or, "I don't want your help," or, "I'll take care of myself." These are the words of a child who is being impacted by trauma and a loss of safety and security in the care of adults. The results are frequently unsafe, inappropriate, misunderstood by peers, and don't get the desired response.

When a child has been impacted by trauma, when their survival skills and defense mechanisms have been engaged and their alert systems have been hypervigilant for months and years, this has long-term effects on development. While other children were learning—to walk and talk, to follow directions and listen, to exercise their skills in math, reading, and writing—the traumatized child was trying to stay alive. Depending on how old the child was when they came to their foster or adoptive home and how many years they lived in unsafe situations, this will correlate with the potential for delays. When a child is living in their survival brain—their lower, base-level functioning brain—they are not able to develop higher brain, executive functioning skills. Our executive functioning skills develop when we feel safe, when our survival brain is disengaged. As long as we feel unsafe and that we need to actively protect ourselves, higher brain development may be delayed.

This is why many adult adoptees are developmentally delayed. Their chronological age does not match their developmental age. They may struggle with mental health issues like depression, anxiety, or even bipolar disorder, in which they have a hard time managing their strong emotions. As the adult adoptee grows and matures, reaching their eighteenth birthday and independence, they may not yet be ready for all that it entails. Parents may feel that their child needs extra time to heal and develop. The adult adoptee may feel ready to fly but still have broken wings. How do parents help and support them while still parenting them?

We have both experienced the launching of children who want to be launched but are not ready. Our children want to be "like everyone else," those who leave for college or move into an apartment. They want to get a job or have an adult romantic relationship. They may accept our continued parenting, or they may reject it. They may stumble and fall, giving us the opportunity to continue teaching them about decision-making and problem-solving. It can be hard to watch our children struggling, seeing them face the world alone when we know they are not yet fully equipped. In the chapters to follow we will explore many different challenges we have personally faced with our precious children and share how we stayed connected while supporting them.

I (Elaine) often joke that adoption trauma hadn't been invented yet when I adopted my children thirty years ago! What I mean is, there weren't yet resources for understanding how to parent differently while realizing the grief and loss your child has experienced. I started changing my parenting when my oldest children were fifteen and thirteen years old. There was a lot to redo! Taking the steps to connect with empathy is invaluable, even in adulthood. It's never too late!

Foundations of Healing

Teaching a child to trust, to use their voice and see themselves as valuable and precious, begins with being a safe adult. A safe adult is someone that is emotionally regulated, calm when their child is not, modeling de-escalation, and helping the child learn to manage their emotions. It involves being attuned to the child—that is, meeting their needs consistently. The child may no longer express their needs. Parents may have to learn the child, recognizing the need before the child can express it or attempt to meet it themselves, perhaps inappropriately or through dysfunction.

Each time the parent meets the child's needs and responds to expressed vulnerability, it reinforces that the child is precious and heard. These attuned experiences are recorded in the child's brain in a new neural pathway, as this is likely a new experience for the child. The more positive experiences there are, the more investment is made in the new groove and the deeper it becomes. With each attuned interaction, progress is made toward changing the child's default belief system. It is important to recognize that the first foundational groove, if established in dysfunction, can take years of investment to change, for this child's trauma-based beliefs dictate behavior and emotional expression. If parents can proactively meet a child's need for attention through connection and love, by pulling them into activities (even if it is folding laundry or cooking dinner), the cycle of the child seeking to meet their own needs can be thwarted and trust can be encouraged.

Loving a child who has experienced trauma is a long road with many twists and turns, and even a few switchbacks. In loving this child, parents are working to heal them of the harm they have experienced. Love is a feeling, but it is more often a choice. Feelings are temporary. They come and go, often lasting only a minute or two before being replaced by another. This is true in any relationship—whether it be marriage, friendship, or even that of a parent and a biological child. No one makes us feel happy and loving all the time. People make mistakes, let us down, or even hurt us. In those moments, love is a choice. We choose to love a person in all their unloveliness. We choose to love the positives and negatives they bring with them, for there is no perfect person. If we have a balanced view of someone then we will acknowledge both sides. Loving them for both sides of themselves is called unconditional love. It involves making a choice to love even when the feelings are absent.

Parents can be detectives of their children. By learning their facial expressions, tone of voice, or body language, parents know they are getting ready to have a hard time. Parents can then meet the need their child has. They may need a snack, a rest period, a hug or connecting touch, or a coping skill. As parents meet needs, as they are attuned to their child, the child will begin to trust the parent and their voice may return as they venture to be vulnerable. In those moments of vulnerability, it is important to be present and responsive to encourage the child to continue using these developing relationship skills.

When parents are meeting the needs of a child, it helps the child to feel safe again. It is not enough for a child to *be* safe; they also need to *feel* safe. They will feel safe when their defense mechanisms and survival skills are disengaged. This happens when a child knows that their needs will be consistently met. When the child feels safe with the adult they are with. When they can find emotion regulation and not be engulfed by their feelings. Establishing these things takes time and commitment. It is important for the child to develop the ability to feel safe in relationships. Parents may find themselves re-teaching relationship skills like mutual respect, meeting the needs of others, the ability to be vulnerable, and trusting others. This is foundational for the child moving forward in order to be able to have healthy relationships in adulthood.

If an adult adoptee, in their transition to adulthood, missed out on any of these developmental goals, there is still time. It is never too late for parents to model and share information with their child, even their adult child. The challenge to the adult adoptee is that without these important life skills in place, they will struggle to find fulfillment and success in life. A lack of healthy relationship skills can manifest in relationships as dissatisfaction, needs not being met, and a lack of vulnerability and trust. Not having healthy social skills can result in difficulty maintaining employment or getting along with others in a variety of settings. Lacking emotion regulation can impact relationships, employment, and general stability. Making sure the adoptee has these skills as they move into adulthood is foundational to their success outside of the home and family.

Good decision-making skills are the last executive functioning skill to develop in the brain, occurring around the age of twenty-five. Prior to that, children and young adults are practicing and honing decision-making skills but are not successful in using them consistently. A child making their own choices independently, to meet their own needs, will often make choices that do not take into account possible consequences or outcomes. Typical young adults aren't that great at decision-making, and the adult adoptee is at a greater disadvantage because of their trauma history.

If parents find that their adult child is struggling in any of these ways, they can always share with their child that they learned something new and want to tell them about it. Psychoeducation can be powerful in helping adult adoptees to better understand themselves and not feel there is something "wrong" with them because they struggle with anxiety symptoms or other maladaptive skills. Helping them to see (if they are open to seeing) that their unhealthy ways of functioning are not their "fault." Parents can normalize that they are the result of the trauma they survived, and this in turn can open the door to teaching them new skills.

If the adult adoptee is not open to learning new concepts in order to bring understanding, then modeling these concepts can still be just as effective. Do not underestimate the impact of teaching through modeling; this is the way most of us learn about these skills initially. Parents can model appropriate social skills and then ask their child to show respect in the same way. Model appropriate emotion regulation skills, staying calm so they can find their calm from your example. Parents can ask their child to walk and talk when they are upset, helping them to see that they calm down faster (because they are burning the adrenaline that is flooding their body). Gift them an alarm clock with relaxing sounds programmed in or a weighted blanket (they are popular for everyone now!). Offer them a stick of spearmint gum when they are feeling low and slow or a piece of bubble gum when they are escalating. Once they are regulated, parents can share this "fun fact" that was just learned about using the sense of taste to regulate. Encourage the child to use it by handing them the rest of the pack of gum. Parents can model appropriate relationship skills by meeting their child's needs, even if they no longer live in the home. Parents can bring a bag of their child's favorite foods each time they stop for a visit or give them gas money when they stop by. Set healthy boundaries and enforce them, modeling appropriate relationships so they know what to expect in other healthy relationships. Parents can simply begin where they are and fill in the gaps they see in their child. These are the skills they will need in order to be successful. It's never too late to start healing!

Parents and Helping Professionals Takeaway

- Attachment begins in utero, so every adopted child has an attachment trauma that may be compounded by other traumas (neglect, abuse, medical trauma, etc.).
- Trauma takes away feelings of safety and security, leaving us with anxiety. This can look like a child who is in fight, flight, or freeze states of mind. Ways to help your child manage anxiety include:
  - Hydration, good sleep hygiene, and healthy nutrition to mitigate the stress hormone cortisol.
  - Regular exercise to burn adrenaline.
  - Engaging the senses in calming activities.
- Control, and the need to have control, is a symptom of anxiety. Instead of power-struggling with your child, power-share instead. This can look like giving choices or reminding them of things they do have control over.
- When a child experiences trauma, they are focused on surviving and may have delayed development. Higher level executive functioning skills only develop when we feel safe and our survival skills are disengaged. Expect delays and plan ways to support them.
- It is never too late! Start modeling emotion regulation, healthy relationships, and social skills today. Share with your child what you are learning and learn together!

Adult Adoptee Takeaway

- When you were separated from your biological parent, an attachment trauma occurred which may impact your ability to trust and feel safe in relationships with your adoptive parents, friends, spouse, or your own children. It is possible to heal and find healthy, secure relationships that meet your needs and allow you to trust in vulnerability.
- Any type of trauma takes away our feelings of safety and security, leaving us with anxiety. Feelings of anxiety can make it hard to function in everyday life. Learning to control the anxiety so it does not control you can help to make work, relationships, and life better. Here are things that can help:
  - Hydration, good sleep hygiene, and healthy nutrition to mitigate the stress hormone cortisol.
  - Regular exercise to burn adrenaline.
  - Engaging the senses in calming activities.
- When we feel anxious, one of the ways we try to feel safe again is by having control over ourselves, our environment, and everyone who comes into our space. It is important to have a balanced view of control. It is not about having none of the control or all of the control. Instead, find the balance between the two. There are some things you do control but there will always be other things you cannot control. You cannot control other people, but you can control yourself. What you control you can problem-solve: Make a plan and work the plan for things to change. What you do not control, you have to accept and then do things that calm your emotions like take a walk, have a bubble bath, or talk to a friend.
- As an adult you may look around and feel like your friends are ahead of you, already doing things you want to be doing. It is important to recognize that the trauma you may

have experienced has delayed your developmental train. You were busy surviving when other kids were learning to walk and talk. You were learning to walk and talk when other kids were learning to run and write. You are on your own path. It will look different than others because it is uniquely yours. Your train is back on the track and it is moving, just give it time to catch up. If you try to rush, hurry, and speed up a train, it has a greater chance of derailing. You are fabulously you! You don't need to be like anyone else!

CHAPTER 2

The Twenties

It might seem curious why the twenties would require their own chapter. Certainly by now adoptive parenting should be complete! However, the twenties are a developmental stage in which adoptive parents will need to connect to their adopted child in a new and different way.

Sharon Kaplan Roszia and Allison Davis Maxon have co-authored *Seven Core Issues in Adoption and Permanency: A Comprehensive Guide to Promoting Understanding and Healing in Adoption, Foster Care, Kinship Families and Third Party Reproduction (Jessica Kingsley Publishers, 2019)*. These core issues are foundational to those of us in the training, education, and work of adoption and foster care. Regardless of how an individual or family has been touched by adoption—whether placing a child, adopting a child, or being adopted—these lifelong complexities have an impact. Regardless of your experience, they apply. Whether you were adopted, fostered, or parented by an extended family member. Whether you adopted or fostered an infant, child, or youth. Whether you adopted from an agency, attorney, facilitator, or from another country. Whether the adoption was open, semi-open, or closed. Whether the loss of the child occurred voluntarily or involuntarily for the birth/first parents. These lifelong core issues will have an impact. It is important for parents and adult adoptees to understand that they are never closed and completed.

They aren't predictive in that they must happen, but they are a great framework to understand what might be going on in the adoptive home. These core issues can be expressed throughout the entire adoption journey but tend to rise up as new challenges in each developmental stage. When adoptees are younger, the adoptive parents are present to guide them through these emotional speed bumps. In their twenties, their parents aren't always the first voice they hear to help them navigate to a safe place.

The Seven Core Adoption Issues
The seven core issues in adoption are loss, rejection, guilt/shame, grief, identity, intimacy, and mastery/control. The adoptee, birth parent, and adoptive parent can experience each of these core issues. Life transitions and life skills that typically occur for the adoptee during the twenties are completing higher education and entering full-time employment (aka, a "real" job), forming adult relationships that lead to commitment, becoming a parent and/or purchasing large items like buying a car or a house. It is clear why this developmental stage would be another season for these core issues to emerge.

Perhaps it is mostly for this reason we felt like this book needed to be written. While many young adults struggle in their twenties, young adult adoptees get tossed back into their adoption issues and in many ways revert to things that they and their parents felt they had already dealt with. When adoptive parents are counseled "you don't get done parenting just because your child is over the age of eighteen," it is often with these core adoption issues in mind.

Loss and Rejection
These are the first two core issues and, for the purposes of understanding the adult adoptee, we will look at them together.

Loss has always been the beginning of the journey. It will be triggered again with change of routine, launching to a new life, and vague feelings of distress and confusion of the unknown future. Rejection comes with that loss as the child wonders "why me?" "What did I do/not do to make this happen?" As rejection becomes internalized it also becomes a protection for further loss, with the thought of "I reject you so you can't hurt me/leave me and allow me to experience overwhelming feelings of loss."

My (Elaine) children have varying levels of struggle with loss and rejection. For one, it was especially tough and it played out in many different ways as she was growing up. She didn't like her birthday. She struggled making good friendships. If she opened herself up as friends do, they would hurt her, so she would rather reject them and play it safe.

In her twenties, she met a good guy and they got married. Like many newlyweds, they needed to start figuring out how they were going to do things as a couple, changing the "me" to "we." When she and her new husband would have an argument, she often wanted to come home. On the one hand I should have been happy because she had spent much of her adolescence wanting to run away from us. Finally, she was running home! Except she wasn't. She was still just running. So, I would say, "I love you. Get back in there and work it out." She would hear through her rejection filter: *They never wanted me, and they are so happy to have me out of the house. I'm not safe out here and now I can't get back.* This was a loss/rejection issue for her stemming from her ambivalent feelings about family, never feeling particularly bonded, then trying to create a new family with a new husband. That was hard!

"If I'm leaving home, is it because I'm being rejected again?" "Maybe they don't want me?" Relationships get complicated when everything is viewed through the rejection/abandonment lens.

Guilt/Shame

Adoptees internalize feelings of worthlessness and hear disappointment underlying every phrase. This internalized feeling of their unworthiness is shame. Whether things are their fault or not, they live with feeling wrong and condemned. This is guilt. This comes out of their sense of loss and rejection.

Sometimes—often, even—twenty-something adoptees make decisions their adoptive parents don't like, and that brings feelings of disappointment. Perhaps their parents really wish they wouldn't have moved in with their boyfriend or girlfriend. Perhaps they dropped out of college and are working several part-time jobs, which feels less than successful compared to everyone else's kids (who appear perfect, e.g., are going to university and have amazing opportunities for career paths that will bring them financial success upon graduation).

This is such a tough situation with an adult child, yet it can be one that allows the adoptive parent to shine their unconditional love best. First, the adoptee knows very well how his adoptive parents feel. He knows their standard. Their rules. Their hopes. Parents can decide the issue won't be brought up every time the two parties are together. Adoptive parents do not have to use every time their son walks in the door to ask him if he has decided to return to college or gotten a real job! Ask him about his day. Learn to know about his life. Offer information about yours. Treat him as a person. As an adult.

Second, the twenties are a great time to correct any misinformation, misperceptions, or mixed messages the adoptee may have about themselves, their story, and the adoptive parent. This is a great time for the adoptive parent to tell their child how proud they are of them and that they are released to make their own decisions.

Then, *do that*. Help them make a plan. One that is healthy, safe, and thought through. They will make mistakes. The adoptive parents' role is to be there to support, guide, and help them recover from mistakes. There will still be those things that aren't okay with the standards of the family. But if they keep coming around, that is just another opportunity to demonstrate the love of Jesus to your child.

This was a struggle for me (Christina). My daughter, in her prodigal journeys, has made many choices I could not support or express approval of. I was tempted every time I saw her to bring them up and talk about them. I had to be mindful of what I was bringing to my interactions: my voice quality, facial expressions, and mood. I had to be purposeful in finding other topics to talk about, other choices to praise her for. And there *were* others, I just had to choose to look for them and see them. I had to take my eyes off of what was important to me in regard to my values and personal beliefs. I instead had to choose to see my child through eyes of unconditional love. This was, and still is, a challenge. Unconditional love is not easy. It takes intentional understanding and practice, but it's necessary because it communicates, "I love you and you are precious to me *no matter what* you do, say, or choose."

Grief

The level of grief is high for adoptees and their parents. There is an underlying sadness for some that defies explanation. Acknowledging the loss and making room for the grief work is the first step toward healing. Lingering questions about birth family may become more pronounced as adoptees leave their home to join with another and make a new family. Adoptive parents need to grieve that this family might not look like they thought or dreamt it would.

Grief work is an individual, complex process. Healthy grieving is cyclical and can be triggered often. The grieving process cannot be shortened or lessened. Grief is about acceptance, patience, adaptation, forgiveness, and endurance.

I (Elaine) have had to work through my own grief with my life not turning out the way I expected. It doesn't go away. Recognizing the loss, processing it with someone trustworthy who gives it validation, then creating ways for coping when the next wave hits, allows me to live a life that is joy-filled and gracious. I need to have that foundation if I want to be the parent that connects with my adult children.

During a recent Mother's Day when I (Christina) could not be with my daughter or mother to celebrate the holiday, I made alternative plans. I went to a hotel at the beach and spent the weekend grieving the loss of what I ever thought motherhood would be. All the expectations, the happy family pictures in my head, everything that I had hoped and dreamed for decades. I released it and let it go. For this was not my reality. In grieving the loss of what was never to be, it opened the door for me to find joy and fulfillment in what was. I was able to lower the bar of expectations for my family and enjoy who my daughter really was. Taking the time to grieve opened the door to healing.

Identity

In their twenties, most young adults are trying to figure out who they are. Biological children may seem to have it a little easier because genetics can help push them in a certain direction. Adoptees have been trying to find themselves for a long time and now the question of "what do you want to be when you grow up?" is staring them in the face.

Many adoptees use this time to search for their biological relatives. With genetic testing and interest in family trees, it is becoming easier to connect with biological family members. Adoptive family members support the journey because it doesn't always turn out the way the adoptee hopes it does. Having someone beside them with a forever attachment will steady the ride.

(Elaine) Two of my children were in their twenties when they did birth family searches. The need to know and understand where they came from was strong, even though their reasons were different. Having biological children of their own gave one a strong curiosity about their own medical history; the other desired connectedness to a greater something in history. My other two children had more openness in their adoptions, so there wasn't a need to search. But my and my husband's attitudes toward birth family remain the same. We have never been threatened by the thought of our children connecting with biological family members. We feel secure in our role in their lives and if additional characters can bring wholeness to them, then we are happy to be part of that journey.

Intimacy and Relationships

When adopted children are little, some of the attachment games played in therapy are for them to look into someone else's eyes and mimic their movements, or to feed each other, or to put Band-Aids onto someone else's "booboo." We play board games as a family and we stress whose turn it is, to share. We live together.

The "baby" therapy games take on new meaning in dating and in more mature relationships. Adoptees struggle with intimacy and relationships when they haven't learned reciprocity or how to "take turns." Are they able to care for each other and meet each other's needs? Do they trust someone else to do that for them? Can they share space? Sometimes they are "looking for love in all the wrong places," trying to fill the void in their heart. This promiscuity can lead to sexually transmitted diseases, pregnancies, and early parenthood. They may hold themselves back, not getting close to anyone, being loners, objects of bullying, and lowering the capacity for intimacy. Sometimes, often due to their history, they may experiment with sexual orientations or identities, looking for belonging and somewhere to fit. Pornography addiction is often seen in adult adoptees because it is a way of feeling connected without needing a real person or relationship.

Attachment and bonding issues find their way into dating and marriage for adult adoptees. For the adoptee who does get into a committed long-term relationship or marriage, they have a new arena in which to learn new skills for trust and attachment. If their partner is skilled and wise, healing can continue to happen, and triggered responses can decrease.

(Elaine) One of the most beautiful things I have been able to observe is my daughter becoming a mother. Given my understanding her attachment issues from being adopted, watching her parent her children causes my heart to overflow with joy! She is so attuned to their emotions and sensitive to their needs. She is building such healthy relationships with them. Having children has been healing for her in many ways because she has been able to process her own birth story.

Control Issues

Power struggles are one adoption issue that never lets up, or at least, not without a lot of work! As was mentioned in the trauma chapter, some of this is because of the broken trust cycle. The adults did not respond to the child's needs; therefore, the child is responsible for himself, and he sees the world as unsafe. He needs to be in charge because only he can be trusted. In our conversations with adoptees, the feeling of loss of power also stems from the lack of choice or lack of voice. As it was explained to me (Elaine) from one of the young people I was working with, "I didn't choose to be adopted. My parents act like it was this big happy day because I guess it was, for them. But for me it was the worst day of my life. I lost everything. Nobody asked me what I wanted." In this situation, her birthmother made an adoption plan because she thought it was the best option for her child. The adoptive parents made the choice to be adoptive parents because they thought it was the best option to grow their family. But no one asked the young adoptee her opinion, because she was a newborn, and she was angry.

These attitudes can manifest in the adoptee as a child who is never going to let anyone else be in charge of her again, wanting to be in charge until her dying breath. Or the adoptee as a child who doesn't care because "what does it matter anyway," he has no influence. Either way, the cause-and-effect continuum has been broken for them. Life feels haphazard and out of control.

This is challenging for an adoptive parent with an adult child in their twenties. The adult child who wants to have all the control can dredge up memories of toddlerhood with their "I'll do it myself" attitude, but they are careening toward disaster with higher stakes. They no longer have household consequences but rather face larger, community-sized consequences.

At one point my husband and I (Elaine) made the decision that our son needed to live elsewhere. His mental health issues were becoming too much for us to maintain in our home environment and we needed another option. We needed to be careful how this was communicated to him because he could easily interpret it as us "kicking him out" when that really wasn't our intention. We also knew he wasn't going to be able to maintain himself in a typical moving-away-from-home arrangement.

Using community support services, he moved into a nearby apartment. It was a great arrangement because he was allowed much more freedom than he had at home with us, yet it was close enough for us to stay involved. However, he really struggled to allow those supports. His thinking was that none of his friends had supports; he should have been able to be in charge and do it himself. He thought he shouldn't have to take medication. He believed that was us trying to control him. After several disasters and missteps that were mitigated by us remaining involved and supportive, and his adult support services being intact, he started to realize he needed those supports. We would talk through it with him. "Did you see how this went better when you had this support in place?" "Did you see how Dad talked to the landlord so he didn't evict you? That was Dad negotiating for you because he cares about where you live and didn't want you to be home-less." We continually have to reframe his thoughts so that he understands what is his to control and what is not.

There must be room for failure in the twenties. Not all kids should or need to go to college. Not all kids need to move out right away. But just as in any other stage, plan for success. As our last child enters her twenties and our first child exits them, we are reminded that it was our faith through it all that kept us steady. We balanced each other and agreed on how we would respond to each of our adult children's needs. We kept our boundaries, but as often as we could, lovingly supported each of them. We were consistently expressing, "We are doing this because we love you and we are your forever mom and dad."

Remembering these core issues and the role they play can help us navigate transitions in the twenties. What is possible for your family? It's a great decade for new things, and adoptive parents can be there to support their adopted adult through it!

Parents and Helping Professionals Takeaway

- The seven core adoption issues are cyclical and will continue to repeat throughout your and your child's lives.
- Loss and rejection are ever-present feelings for your child, so we must choose our words and how we frame things (like launching) with this in mind. Also, think about how you may experience feelings of loss and rejection yourself as your child launches and starts making choices that may be different than what you hoped for them. How do those feelings you experience impact how you feel about and have a relationship with your child?
- Guilt and shame are often experienced when our kids look around and see that they are not living up to our "standards" or "dreams" for them. We need to remember that this is their journey and we are there to walk beside them and support their dreams. Monitor how you feel about your child's choices, if you feel they are a reflection on you and the ways others view your family, and how this may impact how you feel about and relate with your child.
- Grief is something that both you and your child are experiencing. Often this grief can co-mingle with you responding to your child out of your grief and disappointment that life and this family did not turn out how you expected it to be. When your child is also responding out of their grief that they have lost biological family, this can become combustible. Remember to make time to grieve your losses-they are valid and deserve time and space in your mental and emotional self. Often grieving the loss of what you thought this life and a family would be opens the way for healing to begin. Then expectations can be released and adjusted, better reflecting reality and resulting in more peace and calm for everyone.

- Identity is a search that starts in the teen years and carries through young adulthood. Supporting this search and being the soft place to land if it does not turn out the way your child thinks it will help them find trust and safety in their relationship with you. Consider how this impacts your identity and how you see yourself. Do those feelings impact how you interact with your child?

- Intimacy and relationships take flight during the twenties with dating, marriage, and starting families. Many of our children will think about their own birth story when holding their own child. They may struggle to have healthy relationships. We can continue to model this and encourage them to find their way to secure attachment. How is your relationship with your child? Can they use it as a healthy model to build relationships with others?

- Control issues are ever-present. We can remember to power-share and give choices if our child still lives at home or frame their control over their choices (and the rewards and consequences that comes with responsibility) for them. Think about how issues of control also impact you within your relationship with your child. Are you continuing to power-struggle with them? Is this helping or hurting the relationship? Are you power-sharing? How does your child respond? How do you respond when you feel like you are not in control of the relationship (because you are not! You control yourself but you cannot control your child)?

Adult Adoptee Takeaway

- There are seven core adoption issues that many adoptees and their birth and adoptive parents work through over and over again. These are themes that can carry through your life, and being aware of them and how they are impacting you can help you make different, informed choices when they surface.

- Loss and rejection can feel like they are always with you. It is important to remember that these feelings may be deeply rooted in you, but that does not mean you are being rejected by those around you. When any of us experience those feelings, we have to compare them with logical fact by looking around and assessing each situation or relationship individually. Feelings of loss may surface with each new milestone you reach; you may wish that other family members were there to see it. It is important to take care of those very real feelings when they surface and talk to someone you trust about how you feel.

- Guilt and shame can show up and make you feel like you are not enough or not good enough. Remember you are precious—God says so! And your path does not have to look like anyone else's. It is your path, and you can decide which turns you take and where you end up. You have control over that and can make your life what you want it to be.

- Grief is something that can feel overwhelming. Thinking about the things that you lost can cause you to feel sadness and anger that seem to always be present. You have good reasons to be feeling these emotions and one of the most important things you can do is to take care of these emotions when they surface. You can't shorten the grieving process but when you lean into it and take care of the feelings through coping and calming, you can make room for joy.

- Identity may be something you struggle with, especially as a young adult. Wanting to know who you are and where you came from are important questions. You may be able to find those answers. They may help you or they may confuse or disappoint you. Or you may not be able to find those answers; this may frustrate and disappoint you. Remember to care for the emotions that come from this search, in whatever form they take. And remember to lean into supportive relationships that can provide you comfort and that remind you who you are—often, this can help you to find your real identity. You get to make choices about your identity, to become who you want to be.

- Intimacy and relationships are *big* topics in your twenties as you start having adult relationships with higher expectations and responsibilities. Remember you have people in your life who have had adult relationships for decades and can show you the way: your parents! Interview them about what works and what doesn't work. Ask them questions and listen to learn important tips for healthy relationships. Most parents are happy to sit with you and talk about having fulfilling and satisfyingly secure attachments.

- Issues of control can feel ever-present—because they are. Remember, when others have had control of your life and made choices that were hard for you (like in your adoption), a natural reaction is to want to have lots of control over your life so you can feel safe. There are lots of things you have control of, and you can make choices to bring change to your life. However, there will always be things you cannot control, such as any other person you have a relationship with. Trying to control and change things you have no control over is frustrating and exhausting. Try focusing instead on bringing change to the things you do have control over. That is where you can change your life the most.

CHAPTER 3

Trust-Based Relational Intervention

rust-Based Relational Intervention (TBRI)® was developed by Drs. Karyn Purvis and David Cross at Texas Christian University's Karyn Purvis Institute of Child Development. For more than twenty years, they have been researching, studying, and developing programs for children who have experienced trauma, especially attachment trauma. Christina is a TBRI practitioner and we have both been using TBRI principles and interventions not only to relate to and build relationships with our own children, but also in talking about them with the families we work with.

As explored earlier, all adopted children have been exposed to some trauma. For the child adopted at birth, an attachment trauma was created when that child was separated from the biological parent. Trauma could also have been experienced in utero when the biological mother experienced high levels of stress or substance abuse. For the older adopted child, whether adopted from foster care or an overseas foster or orphanage setting, there are additional traumas including possible abuse or neglect. When abuse and neglect occur in the life of a child, these traumas most likely happen within a relationship with their primary caregiver, which impacts the child's ability to feel safe in relationships. Complex trauma occurs when there are multiple traumas that are compounded. This makes it difficult for children to trust adults, parents, authority figures and others.

TBRI addresses how to connect to, empower, and correct children with the trauma in mind while teaching and/or showing ways for parents to build healthy, safe relationships. Many adoptive parents have been using TBRI as their children grow, but can they continue to use it into the young adult years? Absolutely! In this chapter we will explore how to take those principles and continue to use them with the adult adoptee. These principles are instrumental in forming healthy relationships, both for those with trauma and those without. They help children, teens, and adults and are relevant in many spaces, including in the ways parents continue to connect to their young adult children.

Connecting principles are a set of skills that help us to develop relationships with our children that are based in safety, security and trust. These principles include being self-aware as a parent and knowing your own attachment patterns and how they impact the relationship. This awareness is still needed in the relationship with a young adult child. Parents can think about their own attachment journeys into young adulthood. What did you learn about relationships in your twenties? Maybe you learned that other people do not have relationships in the same way you do. Maybe you realized you had an insecure attachment. Perhaps that provided motivation for you to learn about relationships and make changes that moved you toward secure attachment. Maybe it didn't. Maybe it provided frustration and disappointment in relationships. The important reflection point is to look back on your own journey and think about how it may be impacting the present relationship with your child.

When a child was younger, parents may have focused on engaging them with healthy physical touch. Parents may have given the child a hand massage or placed a hand on their arm while they were recounting a hard day, or parents may have played sports and games with their teenager that allowed for safe physical touch. Parents can continue this as they move into the young adult years. When the adult adoptee comes over for dinner, invite them to a game of hoops in the driveway while dinner is cooking. Offer them a hand massage after dinner. Parents can find creative ways to engage their adult child with healthy physical touch, even if it is a welcoming embrace as they arrive and farewell hug as they leave.

Eye contact can be more challenging with young adults but being creative and having fun engaging them in this way can create connections. A parent's vocal quality can also be engaging to the child. Parents keeping the lilt in their voice while offering a lighthearted welcome as their child arrives can engage them in a good visit. Asking questions about their life with curiosity instead of judgement is an example of good vocal quality. When speaking on the phone or in person, monitoring the quality of their vocal tone is one thing parents can become aware of that will help a child feel accepted and loved. Does the parent see their child as precious? Does the child know it? How does the parent communicate it?

Remember that facial expressions are often the first thing someone notices about a person, before they even hear their voice. Monitoring facial expressions can be as easy as looking in the mirror and pretending to greet a child or role-playing a hard conversation with them. What does that face say? Is the face in the mirror smiling, grimacing, or pouting? This will be the face the adult adoptee sees during the conversation, and it can impact whether they share their vulnerable emotions with their adoptive parent. The adoptive parent is working toward ensuring that their now adult adopted child feels safe emotionally.

My (Elaine) children are very sensitive to our facial expressions—my husband would say overly so! When he is thinking hard and trying to follow what someone is saying, he looks very stern. One child exclaimed, "I can't even look at you because every time I do, all I see is disappointment! And I don't even know what I'm doing that is disappointing!" At that moment, he was just trying to listen well! Even when our children become adults, keeping our eyes soft and our tones gentle can go a long way toward maintaining healthy connections with them.

Behavior matching is another tool that can be used to connect to the adult adoptee. Lean in when they lean in. Parents can put a hand to their chin when the child puts their hand to theirs. Mirror and match them to communicate that they are seen and heard. This can be true in playful interactions as well. Take the lead from the child: When they are lighthearted, parents can be lighthearted too. When they are playful, parents can be playful with them. Not every conversation needs to be a serious one. Having fun together, laughing with one another, and smiling at each other all build strong connections.

As parents, we want to empower our children to know themselves and their bodies and to be able to meet their own needs. This includes using their voice to let others know what their needs are. These needs can be physical or emotional. One of the largest needs our children may have is for control, because of their traumatic experiences. TBRI ® Empowering Principles are used to help children have some control over their lives in order to feel safe. Parents can continue to use choices and compromises they've learned through Empowering Principles with adult adoptees. When parents are planning family gatherings or making family choices, allow the young adult to have a say. Can they have the ability within the family to make choices about holidays, dinners, or vacations? Maybe they can choose how long to stay or whether to attend, or when and where to meet and spend time together. This is a natural progression as they move into adulthood and are learning to use their voice. As parents allow them more choices and compromises, it can bring healing and balance to those relationships. They have more of an equality within the family system and the relationships shift in equality.

My (Elaine) son, now living on his own with community supports, comes to our house once a week for laundry and supper, followed by a card game before we take him back to his apartment. We have been able to do this now that he is stable enough for a reciprocal relationship. His level of contentment now that he gets to sit at the table with Dad and Mom and be the only "kid" is heartwarming. He will say things like "this is our bonding time!" It has been good for us and a time of healing in our relationship. I can always tell when we are heading for a rough patch because dinner gets cancelled!

Another Empowering Principle is to introduce short "scripts" when speaking to young adult children that can encourage, motivate, redirect, or teach them. As those same words are repeated by the parent over and over again, they can become the adoptee's scripts. The child will hear those words even when the parent is not present. When parents reinforce concepts like coping skills and character, they are speaking them into the life of their child.

When my (Christina) child calls me, upset and yelling, I say, "Take a deep breath and slow down." I am communicating that I am listening and will be able to better hear what is important to my child if she slows down and calms her emotions. When my child enters or leaves my home, I say, "Hello/Goodbye sweet girl." She has begun calling herself a sweet girl because I have been speaking that into her life every day for seven years. She has told me she wants to have it tattooed on her arm so when I have passed away and no one is saying those words to her anymore, she will have a reminder that she is a sweet girl.

My (Elaine) quiet son has deep-running feelings that we never talk about. More than anything I want him to know I am not going anywhere. So, in birthday cards, notes, texts, and emails, I refer to myself as "Your forever mom." One Mother's Day when he gave me a card, I'm sure my heart skipped a beat when he had written inside, "You're my forever mom!"

Empowering Principles can be used when a child no longer lives at home. Parents can create a feeling of safety for their child by being emotionally available and accepting, meeting their need for love and connection. Adult adoptees still need parents to be their safe places, their comfort zones. Can they tell their parents anything? Are parents an open door they can walk through to find a refuge? Remaining nonjudgmental and validating can allow a child to feel emotionally safe and secure with their parents.

Parents can look for the needs behind their child's behaviors and help them find ways to meet those needs. Identifying what need the young adult child is trying to meet through a certain behavior allows parents to stay connected to them and not be distracted by the behavior, which can put distance between the parent and child. Behaviors are often an expression of something deeper within our child. If we become focused on and distracted by the behavior, we miss the opportunity to help our child with the deeper issue.

When my (Christina) child yells at me, I can look for the need behind that behavior. Often, the need is that my child needs to be heard. I can redirect: "Take a deep breath and slow down so I can understand you because I want to hear you." If my child is moving through romantic relationships and introducing me to a new partner every month, I look for the need behind that behavior. I help her to find ways to meet her needs by talking about healthy relationships and getting her needs for connection met.

Parents can meet their child's needs physiologically. Make sure that when they come to visit there are healthy snacks and hydration available when they walk in the door. If you're meeting them out in the community to go shopping, pack a snack and a water bottle for them. Even if they do not want it, simply offering it communicates that the parent was thinking about them and wants to make sure they have everything they need.

I (Christina) have worked with some families who decided that when their child moved out of the house and made poor choices with their finances, they would not be hungry. They decided that their boundaries would be not saving their child from poor choices by giving them money. Instead, weekly, they would drop off a few bags of groceries. Meeting basic needs within any relationship communicates attunement, care, and the person's preciousness.

Notice the adult adoptee's needs for movement as well. Notice their sensory needs and find ways to meet them. Go for a family walk before or after dinner when they come to visit. If spending the day together doing an activity in the community, choose to go swimming, rock wall climbing, or to a trampoline park. Have fun together! Laugh, encourage, and smile at each other. This brings us back to the Connecting Principles. While meeting the child's needs for sensory input and self-regulation, give cues for transitions. When the family dinner is starting, have a ready prompt that is used each time to signal the transition to mealtime. Have a ritual when a visit is coming to an end. The child will then know what to expect and they will be able to adjust to the coming transition.

Correcting our children can be especially challenging as correction can trigger feelings of shame and guilt as explained in the last chapter. Our children can be sensitive to constructive feedback and correction can negatively impact all the investment we have made into connecting. The Correcting principles may not apply as concretely since parents are often no longer correcting adult children. However, some of the principles can still be applicable. Parents can be proactive by continuing to balance structure and nurture. Parents still need to have structure, or boundaries, with the adult adoptee. The child cannot yell obscenities at or hit parents. Parents may not save them from every poor choice they make. There will be structure to the relationship. However, there also needs to be nurture. There also needs to be care, concern, and empathy. Parents can meet needs, offer support, and care about their child's hurts. When parents offer this to their child, it gives the child a foundation with which to mirror these behaviors to others as well. Parents can model the empathic social skills, meeting their child's needs so that they can then recognize and meet those needs in others. This begins building attunement and healthy relationships for the child.

When parents who have been responsive to the adult child do need to correct or redirect them, the same principles can be used. Maybe the adult child stole from their parents. Perhaps they still live at home and are actively using drugs in the home around younger children. There may be times that a correction is necessary. In these cases, parents can continue to use the IDEAL response:

- Immediate. Address it in the moment. Do not wait.
  I just saw my child take money out of my wallet. I walk over to them immediately.
- Direct. Be direct in addressing the behavior. Make eye contact, gently put a hand on their shoulder.
  "I just saw you take the money from my wallet."
- Efficient. You do not have to have a long conversation. Keep the redirection short. The key is to not escalate the situation further. Yelling and telling your child what a disappointment they are for taking your money not only escalates the situation but also ruptures the connection you have with your child.
  "When you take money, it makes it hard for me to trust you."
- Action-Based. Have them replay or "redo" the behavior/correction.
  "Please put the money back in my wallet. If you need money and ask for it, the answer may be yes. Do you want to try asking?"

- <u>Leveled at the Behavior.</u> Your child is precious even when their behavior is not.

  "I love you and I want to be able to trust you. Your needs are also important to me."

The other important thing to remember, especially in having an efficient response to the adult child, is for parents to monitor the level of their own response so it does not further escalate the situation. If a child takes money from a parent's wallet, there are several responses parents can have—but the child will most likely mirror the parents' response. If parents begin to yell, the child will yell. If parents stay cool, calm, and collected, the child may too. The key is to be attuned to the child, in tune with them, to notice where they are so the parent can engage with them at that level and not a higher level of engagement.

<u>Playful Engagement Response:</u>
"Hey buddy (eye contact, lilt in voice and arm on shoulder). I just saw you take that money out of my wallet. When you do that, it makes it hard for me to trust you and I want to trust you. Can you please put it back and then come sit at the table and tell me why you need it? I can see what I can do to help you, because I love you, buddy."

<u>Structured Engagement Response:</u>
"David, I just saw you take the money out of my wallet. We have talked about this before. Please put it back so that we can work on building trust and then come sit at the table and tell me what's happening. If I can, I will help, because you are important to me."

<u>Calming Engagement Response:</u>
"Take a couple of deep breaths with me and let's walk it off. (Walking with no talking until your child is calmer.) Want to tell me what's going on? You looked really upset when you realized I saw you take the

money from my wallet. I love you and want to help you if I can but when we get back to the house, I do need you to put the money back."

<u>Protective Engagement Response:</u>
When parents realize their adult child is out of control, is a danger to self or others, they may need to be prepared to call for additional assistance. If an adult child struggles with emotion regulation, then keeping the local crisis response numbers available may be necessary. Having a one-page bullet-pointed description of the child that can be handed to the emergency response personnel can help to de-escalate the situation. Include things like the child's diagnosis (if any), what helps them to calm down, and possible triggers to avoid further escalation. Asking for help to de-escalate a child is something many parents must do, even when their child is an adult. Safety is the priority in those situations. Ensure the safety of everyone involved and then wait for crisis response to arrive before trying to engage the child again. Sometimes just having someone other than the parent talk to them can be calming. See if they will speak by phone to a grandparent, family friend, aunt, or uncle. Debrief afterwards to understand how the situation escalated and to create a safety plan for the family, outlining steps to de-escalation for the future.

TBRI is a way of relating to children who have experienced trauma, regardless of their age or stage. It allows parents to continue to build relationships with their children that are based on trust. If parents have been using these strategies during their children's childhood, they should keep using them into the young adult years in order to stay connected and build healthy relationships with the adult adoptee. Remember, adult adoptees with developmental delays due to trauma are still growing. Their brains are continuing to form well into their young adult years. The average child's brain is not done developing until around the age of twenty-five, so if the adult adoptee's development has been delayed, they may be a few years or more behind that projection. To learn more about TBRI you can go to child.tcu.edu.

Tips for Staying Connected with Your Adult Adoptee

a. Send care packages.
b. Randomly text that you love them.
c. Consider if this "issue" is the hill that you want your relationship to die on.
d. Speak their love language.
e. Remember that your child is precious even if their behavior and choices are not.
f. Join them in doing something they love.
g. Bring them their favorite snack/soap/flowers when you see them.
h. Send flowers.
i. Have a pizza delivered when they've had a long day.
j. Hug them when you see them.
k. Be happy to see them—let it show in your face and voice.
l. Find ways to have fun, play, and laugh.
m. Do a movement activity together (rock climbing wall, take a walk, swimming).
n. Tell them their strengths and talents.
o. Be their safe place, comfort zone, refuge, soft place to land.
p. Ask them how you can help.
q. Love their children well.
r. Remember that they are most likely doing the best they can.
s. Don't forget that they are most likely not where their peers are developmentally.
t. Take good care of yourself! Then you can keep taking good care of them.

Parents and Helping Professionals Takeaway

- When Connecting with your child, focus on:
  - Voice quality
  - Facial expressions
  - Mirroring behaviors
  - Putting down distractions and "tuning into" your child
  - Planning time for playful, fun activities
  - Giving hugs and healthy touches
  - Engaging in eye contact as they will tolerate it
- When Empowering your child, focus on:
  - Meeting their needs emotionally and physiologically
  - Being their safe space
  - Providing healthy snacks and hydration when you see them
  - Planning movement-related activities
  - Looking past behaviors to see needs
  - Using several scripts, that you can repeat regularly, to reinforce relationship and coping
- When Correcting your child, if needed, focus on:
  - Balancing structure and nurture. If you increase boundaries, increase nurturing too!
  - Establishing healthy boundaries
  - Being IDEAL: Immediate, Direct, Efficient, Action-Based, and Leveled at the Behavior
  - Being mindful of engagement response: Playful, Structured, Calming, or Protective

Adult Adoptee Takeaway

- Your parents want to connect with you. Just because you are now an adult and can do many things independently, this does not mean that you no longer need your parents. Families are forever. This family that you find yourself in will not go away because you are grown up and can take care of yourself. That was your parent's role during your childhood: to provide for you, protect you and prepare you to be successful in life. They fed and clothed you, had rules to keep you safe and taught you to do things like laundry and cooking. Now that you can do those things yourself, this does not mean that your parents stop being your parents. Their role has changed. They love you and want to spend time with you. They want to get to know you as an adult. They will be available if you want to consult them or have questions about life. They enjoy your company and may want you to just come have dinner or play a board game. They love you and they like you too!

- Your parents may no longer meet your physical needs for food and shelter if you have moved away from home, but you have other needs that they will meet because they love you. Your emotional needs for love, acceptance, comfort, and connection are just as important as your needs for food and clothing. Having a safe space to return to when the world can be a hard place is something your parents can give you. They can sit with you and problem-solve something that didn't work out how you thought it would. They can brainstorm ideas or help look for an apartment near your new job. They are people who have been successful adults for decades and since you are just starting out in this adult life, they have much wisdom to share! And they probably know you well. They know things that you are good at and things that you struggle with. They can give you honest feedback about the choices you are making and how to recover and rebuild if your plans are falling apart. They want good things for you. They want you to be successful.

- Boundaries are part of every relationship, and you may find that as you grow and mature, your relationship with your parents changes. As you seek independence, your parents may step back to give you that space to grow. It doesn't mean they have left, just that they have given you space that you need to become who you want to be. Parents may have new boundaries about what this new "adult" relationship looks like. You may find that they are treating you like they treat other adults. This is part of growing and changing, and your relationship with your parents will go through it as you transition to adulthood. Part of an adult relationship is that each person gets to have a say about what the relationship looks like. Think about ways that you want to connect and spend time with your parents, then invite them or propose those activities. You get to build an adult relationship with your parents and have some control over what that looks like. They get to have control over their part of the relationship too, so this is where everyone gets to use compromise and sharing to make the relationship work. Remember that relationships are living things and those that are not invested in will wither. Find fun ways to invest in the relationship with your parents and watch the relationship change and grow in lots of new ways!

CHAPTER 4

The Launching

This day is on the minds of adoptive parents and adoptees alike—sometimes with the mindset of "He will be living with us forever!" or "I can't wait to get out of here!" But hopefully, this far into the adoption journey, it has been well noted that preparation and planning can help transitions go more smoothly for everyone. Transitioning out of your home, or "launching," is no different.

There are several scenarios for launching that can involve adoptees. Sometimes launching will be the typical move from home to college and then early adulthood. Other times, the transition might be from child services to adult community supports, and the adoptee will not be leaving home. Other, more heartbreaking scenarios include the adoptee launching of their own accord by running away, deciding they are done with parents, or cutting off their relationships, or involuntary launches such as being kicked out by the adoptive parents. These situations will be discussed in later chapters. The particular focus of this chapter will be on the parental attitudes and actions that can continue to build attachment and relationship while at the same time encouraging developmentally appropriate autonomy and growth.

In the previous section, it was discussed how higher-level thinking skills aren't fully developed until age twenty-five in neurotypical kids. Adopted children who have at minimum attachment trauma and perhaps additional developmental delays will not be ready to move out at age eighteen. Or twenty. Or twenty-two. But they can be challenging to have at home because they desire to be their own chronological age. They may make poor decisions and get themselves into situations with stiffer consequences without understanding why.

I (Elaine) noticed that some of my children could not seem to grasp cause and effect. The universe seemed random, whether it was test-taking (studying = good results) or nutrition (healthy food = feel well). Same with watching what peers were doing. If the friends looked like they were having fun, regardless of the outcome (get in trouble, illegal, immoral, risky, dangerous), the friends were a higher influence than us as parents.

It is at this point that I often hear parents giving up on their adopted children. If the relationship with your child has been characterized by tension, pulling apart, vying for position and control, or when the gauntlet of "It's my life, I'm going to do what I want" (often with added expletives for flavor) has been thrown down, it is tempting to give in. And if, as your child is walking away, she looks back over her shoulder and sees a look of disgust on your face, it will reinforce what she has been telling herself all along: "I'm unworthy." "I'm unlovable." "I'm rejected." "No one wants me."

When we got to these pivotal moments with our children, I would say to my husband, "Do we want to be right? Or do we want to have a relationship?" Sometimes he would mutter that he wanted to be right just once, but he knew that the healing our children needed, even at ages eighteen, nineteen, and twenty, would only come through relationship and consistent attempts at building trust.

When we want to plan for the next level, a great place to start as a parent is with a self-assessment. What are you bringing to the table? What expectations do you have for your child? Does it matter to you how this launching thing turns out? Was leaving home easy or hard for you? What kind of memories are stirred from your own experiences? It is good to start here because you will be able to recognize triggers or strong reactions that may have little to do with your son or daughter.

A great example of this is one mother whose son was in a residential treatment facility his senior year of high school. When all the other mothers were hanging senior pictures on the wall and posting pictures of their children on social media with their prom dates and senior sports nights, she had nothing. She felt empty, raw, and overcome with grief. And rightfully so. She discovered that her sense of loss and failure was hers to own because she was holding her situation in comparison to the shiny stories she saw posted and shared. It wasn't right or fair to lay that at her son's feet. She needed to concentrate on being the best mom for him even though he wasn't living under her roof. She needed to use her energy to demonstrate continued commitment and care.

If you are coming out of tumultuous adolescent years with your child, feeling grounded or prepared for launching could seem out of reach. Remember, it is possible with good supports and a plan. A challenging first step as a parent is shifting from being the adult in charge to allowing your child to live with the consequences of their actions.

When the child is young, the parent takes joy in doing things for their children. It is understood that this is how connection is built. As the children grow, they can start being responsible for more things. That doesn't mean the connection is lessened. Parents can still connect through working together or through the rewards after the tasks are done. Part of preparing for launching is allowing kids to be responsible. The sooner parents can do this in the little things, the better it will be with the bigger things. Children can clean their room, pack their lunch, do their own laundry, complete their homework, remember their gym clothes and their sporting gear. Now, encourage responsibility and allow them to fail. Rooms may get cluttered and stinky. Respond by shutting the door. They might not pack their lunch. Respond by having a good snack or an early dinner when they get home. They might get a zero on an assignment or show up unprepared for a game. That's a life lesson for what happens when a job isn't done. They could end up with pink underwear. It wouldn't be the first time! The connection between parent and child can still happen in the response.

"Wow, I bet that was frustrating."

"What did the coach say about that?"

"Aw, poor dear, I saw your lunch on the counter and knew you'd be hungry! Here's a snack!"

With my (Elaine) husband being a teacher, we knew all the hows and whys, so we nagged and rewarded and punished and took things away when our son wasn't responsible. An ADD diagnosis and medication helped but didn't fix his lack of follow-through. Finally, we got to the point where if we weren't going to walk the homework up to the teacher's desk ourselves, we had to let it go. We didn't yell or get angry at him. We were very matter of fact and explained that this is what happens next. He continued to miss out on opportunities, which made us sad. Yet we couldn't follow him around and run interference for him. There were bigger natural consequences that would be much harder to swallow, like failing or quitting school or being arrested because he did something illegal. We had to let go.

As you examine what you are bringing to the table and conduct your self-assessment, discuss with your spouse or partner what you can and can't live with. What are your "non-negotiables?" These probably aren't new to you as a family, but what might be new is how you will respond when your young adult child brings them into your home. What are your options in response? Non-negotiables in your house will probably be things like drugs and alcohol. Some families will include smoking cigarettes, vaping, and sexual activity. Other families will say they will allow those things in their home because they at least know where their children are.

It is important to think about non-negotiables in advance because it is easy to find yourselves in a messy, complicated, chaotic situation and wonder, "How did we get here?" For example, the parents who have the thirty-year-old living in the basement playing video games and ordering the mom to do his laundry and deliver his dinner on a TV tray did not get there overnight. They didn't make a conscious decision to end up there, but these outcomes can creep up as little things become tolerated and accepted. Parents frequently aren't in agreement about what the rules are, and the child learns very quickly how to play one against the other.

It was hard for my husband and I (Elaine) to decide which things were non-negotiables, which behaviors were truly destructive and unsafe versus ones we just didn't like. For example, tattoos. To my husband, they are horrific: a complete waste of time and money that make no logical sense. In his growing-up years, only the bad kids got tattoos, yet our children have them! And to compound his frustration, the tattoos were paid for by money that should have been coming to us for fuel, cell phone, and car insurance. "Helpful" people would say things like, "I would never let my child get a tattoo," as their eyes glanced over our way. My hackles would raise. I wanted to say, "You just go ahead and *try* to keep a child from doing something!" As if we have that kind of control over another human being! What we did know was that tattoos weren't inherently dangerous or unsafe. While not thrilled, we tried hard not to make the issue a battleground. I took an interest in the designs and meanings of each one.

When our seventeen-year-old wanted a tattoo for his birthday, he tried a different tactic. He saved his money to pay for it himself, asking only for a signature. He put so much time into thinking about what he could get that Dad would find acceptable.

I needed to stay with him in the tattoo shop since he was underage, so that was a bonding experience!

The point of a non-negotiable is that its use is not protected or enabled in the home. The rule is clear. Perhaps for this season, all alcohol is banished from the property, including for the parents' social drinking. If objects or evidence were to be found in the home or cars, the child would be confronted with it before being told once again how much they are loved and valued as part of the family and how scared and worried their parents are about the direction these choices might take them.

The parental response to a young adult child should always be welcoming and warm. Parents must be aware when substance *use* switches to substance *abuse* and when welcoming becomes enabling. Don't give money, especially if it is going to end up being used for drugs or alcohol. Do purchase food or useful items if that's what's needed. If a charge of drug possession occurs, stand beside them, make trips to the courthouse, but don't make excuses. Learn what addiction looks like and be familiar with resources in the community to get help before it is too late.

When preparing for launching, it is imperative that the parent remembers that they are the adult. They have the responsibility to act, think, and make decisions like one. In terms of parenting, that means parents are still the role model in emotion regulation, responding instead of reacting, and working on building a trusting, connecting relationship regardless of the child's age.

TBRI was presented in the previous chapter. A great concept from TBRI that is used to build relationships, develop feelings of safety and security, and decrease misbehaviors is to increase both structure and nurture at the same time. This is so challenging to do! When a parent is angry about a child throwing a toy and breaking a family heirloom, the last thing she wants to do is pull that child close and remind them of their preciousness (while reminding them that toys aren't thrown, so that toy will need to be put away for a little bit)! This flies in the face of common parenting trends. The usual reaction to address misbehaviors is for parents to increase structure (give children a time out, make them sit on a chair, give them extra chores, ground them for a week, withhold their allowance) and decrease nurture (give them the silent treatment, respond with short answers, don't remain in the same room, withhold affection, withhold family rituals). The reverse is also true: When parents want children to feel their love and affection, they increase nurture (buy presents and toys, give in to demands, make their schedule solely child-focused) and decrease structure (limit responsibility, hold no accountability, set no schedule, general nonchalance).

As the adult and parent of the young adult child, who is still responsible to think about building connection and trust, it is imperative to look at ways to increase structure and nurture while launching and transitioning. Structure is increased through increased responsibilities, appropriate autonomy, setting boundaries, and not "doing for them" as much. While this is viewed as healthy and necessary—a step in the right direction toward independence—the young adult adoptee may view it through the ever-present rejection/abandonment lens. "Dad must not want me anymore." "Mom is trying to get rid of me." The adoptive parents will need to be very intentional about increasing nurture while creating boundaries for launching. "I am so proud of you!" "I am your forever mom." "We can do this together."

When my (Christina) daughter launched to an adult group home, I wanted to be supportive of her and her needs, specifically her need for connection. I knew this would be a difficult transition because as much as she said she wanted independence and freedom, I also knew she was not completely ready for everything she wanted. I knew she might not have fully understood how much her life was going to change. I wanted her to be successful, so I made a plan to increase the nurture in our relationship while the structure of her life was drastically changing. I scheduled to visit her every week, talk to her every day, and send her cards and reminders that even though she was no longer living at the house, she was still a member of the family, and our relationship would remain her support.

When my (Elaine) son no longer lived with us, I had a chance to practice increased structure/increased nurture. He was no longer going to be able to stay under our roof. He was becoming antagonistic toward our parenting and homelife was becoming extremely chaotic—not only for my husband and me but also for the remaining children. We found an apartment within three blocks of our home within his price range, and he moved out. He got a lot of support from his community supports provider, and we also kept affirming our relationship. He could walk over to our house for an occasional meal or to do a load of laundry. He knew we were still for him. Occasionally he will say we kicked him out, and I will remind him of his preciousness and value to us; that he is where he needs to be.

It was hard for him because he didn't have all the skills needed at first. He could boil water, which meant he could make spaghetti, his favorite food. He knew how to wash his dishes. But he had a lot to learn about personal safety and relationships, specifically that not everyone could be trusted. Those were hard lessons.

Adoptive parents might need to lower the bar for what skills need to be mastered before moving out. What follows is a list of skills to help you prepare your child for "launching." Working on one at a time can be a good plan that will not be overwhelming.

Independent Living Skills

- Doing laundry
- Basic cooking (knowing how to make five meals)
- Shopping for food and clothes
- Cleaning bathrooms, kitchens, and bedrooms (safely using cleaning supplies)
- Making doctor's appointments
- Getting prescriptions and keeping them in safe places
- Organizing personal information (insurance cards, licenses)
- Keeping track of internet accounts and passwords
- Opening and managing a bank account/debit card
- Communicating and negotiating with roommates
- Knowing how to pay bills
- Traveling using private and public transportation
- Checking email
- Dealing with emergencies: medical, calling 911, weather, car accident
- Taking care of a friend who is in trouble
- Behaving in a sexually responsible way
- Be brave enough to say no, respectfully but forcefully
- Managing/counting money—you can't spend more than you have and when it is gone, there is no more.
- Using a cell phone/house phone
- Asking for and accepting help
- Completing an employment application and hiring paperwork (social security numbers, etc.)
- Navigating directions for walking or driving
- Washing dishes/running a dishwasher
- Setting an alarm/time management/marking and reading a calendar
- Ordering at a restaurant/fast food

- Basic first aid (cough and cold medicine, Band-Aids and antibiotic ointment, Ace bandages, etc.)

The last piece of general launching/transitioning advice to add here is the importance of additional supports. There are many points during an adoptees' endeavors to grow up when they are certain that their dad and mom have no clue what they are dealing with—and aren't trustworthy anyway. They are still acting on their survival skills, not developing healthy relationships or taking care of themselves as they should or were taught to when they were under their parents' roof. If community supports or services based on diagnoses can be accessed in order to provide another voice speaking structure into the young adult's world, it allows the parent to focus on the nurture part. Church and other community groups can get involved, adding another layer of support in the life of the adult adoptee. Extended families are also good for this. Grandparents, uncles, and aunts who are willing to invest in the lives of adoptive families are such a gift and lighten the load of launching. While planning and preparing, don't hesitate to ask and seek out these additional supports.

Parents and Helping Professionals Takeaway

- Make sure that, as parents, you are on the same page. Spend time talking about what it will look like for your child to launch, what you expect of them, what the timeline will be, and what supports you will provide.
- Talk about what boundaries you, as parents, will have. What can you provide without resentment? Think about what you can provide emotionally. Dinner once a week or once a month? At the house or in a neutral space like a restaurant?
- Increase your child's responsibility as they prepare to launch. One responsibility a parent has is to prepare their child to be successful. Part of that is teaching them to make meals, do laundry, use public transportation, etc. As you increase their responsibility, this also builds into their feelings of confidence and competence, that they are ready for this next transition.
- Know the difference between staying connected and enabling. Families are forever. You will always be connected in relationship, and building into that connection is important. Connection, however, does not mean that you are responsible for your child, have to run interference for them, or manage their consequences to make life easier. This becomes a slippery slope toward an enabling relationship. Do not do for your child what they can do for themselves. It is loving to prepare your child to launch, to build into their confidence and competence.
- Remember to balance structure and nurture. As you increase structure and add responsibilities, increase the nurture you are providing as well.

Adult Adoptee Takeaway

- Your parents want you to be successful in life.
- They will teach you many things that you will need to know (cooking, laundry, making appointments and getting to them, etc.). This is because they believe in you!
- Becoming more responsible is part of becoming an adult. Adulthood has lots of privileges but also responsibilities. If being an adult is a scary thing to think about, then this would be a great time to get support from a helping professional to talk about those fears and find ways to manage them. Sometimes we don't feel ready because we aren't done being a kid yet! If you spent a lot of your childhood overcoming trauma or learning to be part of a family, it can feel like you aren't ready yet to move away from your parents. Something that can be scary is feeling like we must learn all adult responsibilities at one time. Your parents understand this and will partner with you to learn them at a pace that feels comfortable but not overwhelming. Communication is important in order to let your parents know how you are feeling about these changes.
- The more you practice being responsible, the more confident and ready you will feel for adulthood.

CHAPTER 5

Loving the Adult Adoptee Well

Adoptive parents love their kids! But does the adult adoptee know it? How do parents express their love to their children in ways the child will see and understand it? Meeting a child's needs, being safe people for them, and creating felt safety in ways that give them a comfort zone and a safe place to return to for refuge are ways that parents can display love. Each child is different and will have different things that communicate love to them. Sometimes it is helpful to ask the child what they prefer in an expression of love. They may respond that they feel loved when parents give them hugs, make their favorite dinner, or praise them for a job well done. These are called love languages.

Gary Chapman wrote the book *The 5 Love Languages* (1992) to explain how we can recognize when others are loving us and love them better by speaking their language. It is important in a relationship to recognize when someone is trying to love you. Maybe they bring you little gifts all the time. A drawing, a flower, a bag of your favorite snack, or a book you were looking for. You may prefer hugs and physical affection, but it's important not to miss the expression of love from a child when they are showing it. In the same way, we can watch someone else to recognize their love language, or the way they prefer to receive love. They may accept your gifts when you bring them but light up when you praise them for their hard work or strengths. Those words of praise may mean more to them than anything else. If you recognize that, you can be intentional about loving them in the way that means the most to them.

The first love language is "words of affirmation." When parents use words to love their kids well, it looks like speaking or writing, in notes or cards, the things the parent appreciates about the child. Parents can identify the child's strengths and talents, a good job they did on a task, or a positive choice they made. They can put notes in their child's lunch if they still live at home, send them daily text messages, or call them and talk to them. This is loving them with words.

The second love language is "acts of service." Parents can show their love through actions. This may look like parents completing a chore for the child occasionally (if they live at home). If a parent knows their child is having a busy week at work, the parent can tell their child that they will drop dinner off on Thursday. Maybe a parent fixes something around their child's house or helps with childcare, if able. Parents using their strengths and abilities to bless their child in a special way can mean a lot to the adult adoptee.

The third love language is "quality time." This may look like spending time with them doing an activity of their choosing. Sometimes just sitting together and having a cup of tea, coffee, or iced tea will help a child to feel loved. If this is the child's love language, they may invite parents to do things with them, such as watching a TV show or movie. This means parents put aside distractions and electronics to be present in the moment, focusing on the time spent with the child and what they are saying or doing.

The fourth love language is "physical touch." For children who prefer this expression of love, they may be constantly finding ways to touch people. They may hang on parents or touch their hand as they are talking. The child is attempting to connect. Parents can give them a hand massage or a back rub. Hugs or holding hands may also be activities that help them feel close and connected. Even if parents are uncomfortable with a lot of touching, if they try to touch their child in ways that are meaningful, it can increase the connection.

The fifth love language is "gifts." This does not necessarily mean parents buy a lot of things for the child. It can mean parents bring something to let the child know they are thinking of them—maybe baking their favorite cookies and bringing them each time they visit. Or perhaps making them something for their home, for their children, or for themselves. Parents can give a container of their favorite lotion or special soap, a shirt that the parent saw and thought they would like, or a blanket the parent made.

Try out each one of these ways of loving the adult adoptee and see which one gets the largest reaction. Look for a smile, the child melting into a hug, or a big "Thank you!" Once you discover the one that most impacts the adoptee, repeat, repeat, repeat!

When my (Christina) daughter came home at the age of fourteen, getting to know her was my most important pursuit for many months. I tried lots of ways to love her to see which one she liked best. She did not enjoy physical touch, even hand massages. She cast aside gifts (I would find them discarded under her bed). The notes I wrote, telling her how much I loved her, ended up in the trash. She did not respond when I did things for her. But when I spent quality time with her, she leaned into it and lit up. When I told her we were going out, just the two of us, she loved it. When asked how she wanted to spend time together, she always chose to sit side by side watching a movie or TV. Just being together, and my being completely focused on spending time with her, brought her contentment and appeared to fill her bucket. It meant that I was intentional about putting aside other tasks and distractions so I could be present. When I did, she would lean into me and let me play with her hair. Those are some of my favorite memories and activities (which she still chooses to do when given a choice).

The five love languages are a great place to start when figuring out yourself, your spouse, and your child! But we also want to encourage you when it might feel like your young adult child doesn't have a love language. It may feel that in the dance you're doing, all that seems to be happening is your toes getting stomped on. It's easier to give up than to keep putting in effort to love them well. Here are a few of our quick love-them-well suggestions that you can do while expecting nothing in return:

- Milkshake date. Thick, creamy, sweet . . . it's sensory and it can't be rushed.
- Car ride to nowhere while your child plays DJ. They can tell you why it's their favorite song (even if they say, "I like the beat," now you know).
- Do something they like, or centered around their interests, for thirty minutes of undivided time. You don't have to like it. You are the adult and can work on tolerating discomfort!

Adult Adoptee, Parents, and Helping Professionals Takeaway

- Loving each other is a *big* part of any relationship. Take time as a family to get to know the preferred love languages of yourself and those around you.
- Recognize when someone is loving you using another love language. It may not be the one you prefer but at least acknowledge that their intent is to show you love.
- Once you know someone else's love language, try to speak it to them more frequently than the other ones. In this way, you will be loving them in a way they can feel deeply.

CHAPTER 6

Challenging Conversations

When an adult adoptee begins stretching their wings and preparing to fly, one of the things they do is to differentiate from their parents. They begin making choices and seeking independence and autonomy. They want to become their own self, to define their identity. This autonomy-seeking can look like pushing away, becoming different from their parents by doing the opposite of what their parents have taught them, or choosing different values than the ones their parents have instilled in them.

It is important for parents not to take these actions personally. The child is not rejecting them, even though it might often feel that way. Instead, the child is trying to find their own identity. If parents can remember this, it can help them to remain the constant safe place that their child needs them to be. When parents feel rejected, their response can be to shut down. However, if they do not personalize their child's behaviors and choices, and choose instead to remain open and welcoming, the child may be able to use their parents as the secure base that they need them to be in order to effectively explore their environment and interact with it.

Equally important is to remember that the adult adoptee, who is becoming independent, is able to make their own choices. It is the expression of their developing identity. In making their own choices, they may make decisions parents do not agree with or feel they can support. Sometimes a child may be trying out different "hats" to see which one feels comfortable to them. Some of those choices are scary to parents: If their children continue down a certain path, parents fear they will become destructive and harmful. When parents respond to a decision that is not one they would have made for themselves, the child loses the safe place the parents might have been able to provide. They will feel rejected, and this can create a wall in the relationship. A child will be less likely to come to their parents with their next decision, whether it ends up being successful or unsuccessful. When the choice is a successful one, parents want their child to bring it to them so they can be part of the celebration. When the choice is unsuccessful, parents want their child to bring it to them so they can be their safe place, a source of problem-solving and learning on how to recover from poor choices. This only happens when parents remain open, accepting, and validating toward their child, when parents look at their child through eyes that say, "You are precious," even if they do not agree with or support the choice. The bottom line is that when the child is an adult, parents do not need to approve of their life choices in order to love them. Adult adoptees get to make those choices, and a parent's job at that point in their child's life is to be the safe place they can come to when the world is a hard place. When the child's poor choice does not work out the way they thought it would, instead of saying, "I told you not to do that," a parent can say, "I'm so sorry that didn't work out how you thought it would. Want to talk about it?" When parents have this approach, they are leaving the door open to be able to provide support to their child even when they do not support their choices.

Secure attachment says, "You are precious even when your choices are not," "You have value even when you make mistakes," and, "I love you even on your worst day." Is that what parents are communicating to their children? It is easy to communicate that on the best days, but when parents can communicate that on their worst days, that is where emotional safety and security in a relationship is found. Are parents offering that to their children? If parents offer nonjudgmental, accepting, and positive regard to their child, the child feels safety. Parents can accept their child without accepting their behaviors and choices. Parents can value their child without valuing their decisions.

I (Christina) experienced this when my daughter began smoking cigarettes. I had a hard time accepting this because my child was obviously trying to fit in with a certain friend group. She would smoke around them but at no other time. I reinforced my boundaries (the same ones I had for everyone else): No smoking in the house or car, and I would not provide money for cigarettes. I did not get stuck on the behavior, and because of that, my daughter and I were able to talk instead about the meaning behind the behavior—trying to fit in and find her place to belong.

The largest challenge for many adult adoptees is the attachment trauma they struggle with. Their insecurity in the parent–child relationship comes to the surface at these times. For the adoptee who already feels different and even disconnected from parents, even if they have worked hard to become securely attached, they are looking for the rejection they believe is coming. They can be hypervigilant to any perception of rejection. A look on their parent's face, a shift in body language, or a change in the tone of voice can be perceived as a clue that parents are rejecting them. Adoptees may then respond by putting up walls within seconds, and a shutdown commences as they seek to withdraw from parents before parents can withdraw from them. They are using their self-preservation skills and defense mechanisms to protect their heart from the pain of perceived rejection.

Adoptees may not naturally turn to parents for support and comfort if secure attachment has not been able to form. They may seek that support and comfort from others, perhaps finding it but oftentimes not, leaving them feeling alone in their poor choices and distress. This can lead to shame and guilt, which builds walls around them that can be hard to scale.

If parents can maintain the light in their eyes when they see their child, the lightness of voice when they say, "I love you," the open arms of a hug when they come through the door, this allows adoptees to feel validated. They can feel loved even when they are struggling or feel like they have let their parents or themselves down. This is how parents can continue to provide a safe place of relationship even if the child no longer lives in the home. Even if parents do not agree with the choices they are making; even if they are bringing problems through the door with them that need to be solved. A child is precious to parents, no matter what!

Having conversations about difficult and challenging topics can be hard. Let's take the rest of this chapter to explore several topics that might be helpful.

Tattoos, Piercings, Haircuts, and the Search for Identity
Adult adoptees can struggle with identity for many reasons. They can be searching for acceptance from many groups of peers; a place to belong. They can be trying to identify with their biological family or history. They can be pushing against morals or standards that adoptive parents have raised them with to test the sincerity of their love. They can be expressing themselves in ways they want others to see.

Regardless of the reason for the expression, parents have a choice to make. Is the choice the child is making (a tattoo, piercing, etc.) going to make or break the relationship? Is this the hill a parent wants their relationship with their child to die on? As much as parents may not like or approve of a decision their child makes, it is their child's decision to make. A parents' role is to continue to communicate that they love their child, that the child is precious no matter what. Adoptees may be looking for a reaction. When there is none, there is no resulting power struggle that can damage the relationship.

In their search for identity, they may try on a lot of "hats" before finding the one that fits. Practicing patience and providing support as they go through this process can maintain a strong relationship that the child can then use as a foundation in their search for identity. Being nonjudgmental and unconditional in support of them as a person is the key to protecting the relationship parents have been building with them over the years.

My (Christina) daughter wanted a piercing. I didn't feel like it was a good idea because I knew she was not responsible enough to take care of the cleaning and care instructions after the actual piercing. We made a compromise: I would not pay for it, and she would get a job for the summer to earn the money for it. When she had the money, we went and got the piercing. A week later, the piercing was infected. We went to the doctor, and, after two rounds of antibiotics, she had to have the piercing surgically removed. I was able to remain her soft place to land as I said, "I'm sorry that did not work out how you thought it would." My daughter learned an important lesson and has not asked for another piercing since. She now also knows it would be hard for her to care for, but it wasn't me telling her that. She found out for herself, and that was more meaningful for her than a power struggle with me ever would have been.

Dating, Sexuality, and Pregnancy

Part of attachment trauma can be insecure connections. When an adult adoptee begins to seek love outside the family, it can look chaotic and anxious. They may seek one relationship after another, unable to tolerate being alone. Their lack of trust and anxiety in the relationship may place stress and pressure on their partner, causing those relationships to be tumultuous or short-lived. It can be hard for parents to watch all of this from the sidelines as their child struggles. However, if parents can be a safe place, then they can be the stable relationship the adoptee can come to when their world is hard. When a child can come to their parents in their pain and vulnerability—and if parents can remain cool, calm, and collected about the dysfunction of the child's relationships—they will take lessons away from every relationship experience. It is a learning curve for the adoptee. Meanwhile, parents offer comfort and support to help their child problem-solve what didn't work about the situation and what they can take away from it. This can be instrumental in helping the adoptee move forward to healthier relationships. It is crucial not to get stuck on the situation itself but to stay focused on offering comfort and support to your child.

One thing parents can focus on and impart to their child is the healthy development of a relationship. Talking to the adoptee about the steps of building healthy attachment in a nonjudgmental and information-sharing way can give them the building blocks to create better connections. As our adoptees enter the age of wanting relationships, we find they are more willing to listen because they are curious about, and want to have, good relationships.

It begins with attunement—determining if the person they are starting a relationship with meets their physical and emotional needs. Good relationships are mutual and reciprocal. A nice reminder of this is how we take turns and share. Is the adoptee only allowing others to take care of their needs, or are they reaching out in mutual respect and care to meet the needs of their partner? This is an important, foundational step to building a healthy relationship.

Helping a child learn to recognize trustworthiness in others can help them have more stable relationships. Sharing emotions should happen when a relationship is a safe place and provides a comfort zone. When trust is present, it calms anxiety. This leads to vulnerability and the ability to share the true self. This is when and where someone can express their innermost thoughts and feelings. When adoptees, in their anxiety about keeping the relationship, share their emotions too early on, this can be damaging both to the connection and to the child. The partner in the relationship may feel overwhelmed and take huge steps backwards, even out of the relationship. When the adoptee shares their heart without trust being present, they are not protecting their heart, placing them at a larger risk of being heartbroken. Talking through these steps with the adoptee, helping them understand how to build a strong and healthy relationship, improves their success and their self-confidence.

When the adult adoptee is sexually active, whether parents agree with their sexual choices or not, making sure there are conversations about sexual safety is important. The adoptee can want to please others or may be more trusting of others, whether they know them well or not. As a result, they may be more vulnerable to being used or abused. Talking to the adoptee about consent and the importance of protecting, not only their hearts, but their bodies as well is a way parents can support their child in their journey. Communicating that a parent's love and care for their child means they want that child to be safe is a way to stay connected during these years. Taking time to talk about the difference between safe and unsafe relationships—including the need for respect, compromise, and feeling seen and heard—can lay a foundation for future relationships. For the child who has sexual and physical abuse in their history, it can be empowering for them to realize they get to have control over their bodies and who has access to them. They may not realize this until you share it with them, but it is so important for the child to know.

Pregnancy can be a trigger for the adoptee because it can transport them back to thinking about their own start in life, their relationship with their biological parents, and the losses they experienced. They may need their adoptive parents' support at this time especially, both to manage their emotions and create a cohesive narrative about their life story. Narratives can be very helpful in the healing journey. Seeing life as a story that continues to evolve and develop can reinforce many important concepts: The story is not finished; there is more left to be written. The future remains unknown, and the adoptee has some control over how it goes. Adoptees may not have had control over their childhoods, which were characterized by trauma, but they do have control over their own child's childhood. This can be empowering for some adoptees and anxiety-producing for others. Parental support during this transition to parenting can help the adoptee break the cycle of abuse and neglect that may have started their story. Modeling (by interacting with grandchildren, creating secure attachments, showing unconditional love, and practicing trust-based parenting) can help the adoptee learn ways they can parent well.

My husband and I (Elaine) felt strongly about sexual purity for our children, not because we saw sex as something to be ashamed of, but rather we viewed each of our children as created in the image of God and so very precious! We didn't want anyone to take advantage of them or use them in a way that could hurt them. Our understanding is that sexual intimacy is part of a greater emotional intimacy that takes place in healthy, mature, reciprocal relationships and is more than just a physical connection. We were attempting to protect them by teaching about purity. They were worth being treasured, cared for, and lavished upon!

Sadly, that isn't what they heard. Now that I know more about adoption trauma, I can understand. They applied all their filters and heard: "My parents don't trust me," "My parents are trying to control me," "My parents don't understand; this person really likes me," and, "My parents don't know what they are talking about." Because of these alternate messages, our children did make choices we didn't like. But our message stayed the same: "You are precious!" "You are worth being treasured and lavished upon." "You are worth being treated well." "You are worth being cared for."

Drugs and Substance Abuse

When adoptees who have experienced trauma become teenagers and young adults, substance abuse can become a challenge the family faces. When a person experiences a traumatic event, it leaves them feeling strong emotions of sad and scared that, if not calmed, will grow into the secondary emotion of anger. These powerful emotions can feel overwhelming and uncomfortable. When control of these emotions has been lost, there is a desire to get control back to restore balance. If adoptees have not learned how to cope with and calm those emotions in healthy ways through emotion regulation, then they are more likely to use and abuse substances to find that control. If adoptees have felt overwhelmed by emotions for years, then a peer offering them a substance that will help them to find feelings of calm and peace will sound like a tool that is too good to be true. And it is too good to be true, because a lifetime of addiction is the risk. If adoptees can find peace and calm by controlling their emotions using substances, then each time the substance brings that calm, a groove or neural pathway is created in their brain that says, "This is how we control emotions and feel better."

Understanding this, how can parents support their children in this space? Parents can help them in the teen years to find emotion regulation, to learn healthy coping skills for their feelings. Encouraging adoptees to engage in therapy where a lot of those skills are learned can be a great support to them. Introducing healthy emotional expression and calming in the family can be a support to them too. Taking family walks in the evening or playing basketball in the driveway to expend the adrenaline that has been building up through anxiety response; listening to music and singing along while driving; chair dancing and giving expression to emotions can calm big feelings. Encouraging adoptees to write in a journal, and then respecting the privacy of that space so they can feel safe to write anything they are thinking and feeling, can de-escalate emotions. Doing progressive muscle relaxation and stretching as a family to practice breathing and centering activities can help the adoptee to find their calm and peaceful feelings. Building into this before and during the teen and young adult years is preparing the adoptee for success to avoid substances.

However, if a child has begun using substances and is experiencing addiction, it is important for parents to think about their own boundaries. One healthy boundary is to not do for your children what they can do for themselves. Determining whether a young adult is using substances or abusing them and dealing with an addiction is an important first step. Often substance users must hit rock bottom before they are ready to try something new. That may mean a criminal charge or losing their home.

It is important for parents to determine what their boundaries are and where they stand before having to enforce them. Creating boundaries in the moment is nearly impossible because emotions are high, and parents may be making serious boundary choices based on the emotional brain instead of the logical brain. When a child first begins to struggle, sit down as parents and determine what the boundaries will be and how they will be enforced. Then, in the hard moments, you will already know your plan of action and will not have to sort between emotions and logic. Having boundaries allows parents to provide support while being comfortable and confident with their choices. It allows parents to protect themselves from being used and abused by someone who is not making good choices because of their substance abuse. It allows the child and their choices to be separate from parents and their choices. Parents' boundaries are what often cause a substance abusing child to seek help and get serious about treatment. Stepping in to rescue and save them from hitting rock bottom is enabling them to continue the addiction cycle. Allowing them to face the consequences of their actions is a loving approach as a parent. The hardest part is watching a child go through the hard consequences of their choices. It is also critical for parents to not deny what they are observing, but to be very realistic. If money is disappearing from the house, if paraphernalia is found, face this head-on instead of waiting to see if things will get better. In this situation, it is the role of the parent to be the supportive, soft place where the child can land. That does not mean they must land at the parent's house! It does mean, however, that parents can approach adoptees with an accepting and nonjudgmental attitude. They can accept their calls. They can bring them something to eat. They can sit in the courtroom at their hearing. They can offer them hugs and love. Parents can let their child know that they are precious, they are loved no matter what, and they are not alone (which is often their largest fear). Parents can continue to extend unconditional love. "I love you no matter what." "I may not support your choices, but I support you." Being able to separate the child from their behaviors and choices is imperative to providing this support. The child remains precious even when their behaviors are not.

Money Management and Employment
Another challenging conversation where boundaries are beneficial is regarding money and finances. Adoptees need parents to teach them about budgeting and how to manage their money. This is an important life skill that can be complicated by trauma-impacted developmental delays. If an adoptee's brain development has been impacted by early childhood traumas and their executive functioning skills are delayed, they may have a harder time with impulsivity or poor choices. Executive functioning skills include organization, time management, self-control, emotion regulation, working memory, focus, planning, flexibility, goal setting and achievement, observation, stress tolerance, and initiative. Managing finances involves almost all those skills. Using self-control to save money and plan how to spend

it, staying flexible when unexpected costs arise, setting goals for saving, and remembering what bills need to be paid first are all skills that lead to success. However, if the adoptee's executive functioning skills are taking a little longer to develop than others at similar chronological age, this can cause failures that impact a child's confidence.

Explaining healthy money management is the first step. When parents teach their children about the value of money, beginning with an allowance and earning money for chores, this reinforces a work ethic. Parents can invite them to observe paying bills so they can understand the operating costs of a home. Talking to them about what parents are saving for and how to set aside money sets a foundation for them to build on themselves. Modeling is the best teacher. Talk to them about what they plan to do with the money they are earning from their first job—even if it is babysitting or lawn mowing. Have those conversations openly and honestly because every input into the groove for money management deepens the pathway until it becomes the default. Each mistake or poor choice they make (when parents do not shame but instead show them how to problem-solve) becomes a learning experience. It gives the decision-making part of their brain exercise and practice until it is competent.

It's important to come alongside the child and help them when poor money choices lead to consequences. When they impulsively spend their savings and have no funds to pay the monthly bills, what will parents do? When they have large college bills and student loans to pay back but use their savings to buy a brand-new car with no job lined up, how will parents respond? Having boundaries—knowing what they are and how they will be reinforced before you need to use them—will increase confidence in the moment. Similarly, just as with children who abuse substances, hitting rock bottom financially can be a great learning experience. It may make a large impression that will inform all the child's choices moving forward. Parents may not save their children by providing financial assistance to save them from consequences, but they can problem-solve with them. Parents can help children brainstorm solutions and create a plan. They can then encourage adoptees to follow the plan. They can be their cheerleader.

When adoptees are looking for and securing employment, they may struggle to maintain it (again, based on those delayed executive functioning skills). Undeveloped time management skills may mean they are late to work and their job is in jeopardy. Getting them watches with alarms or helping them to set alarms on their phones can be helpful. Organization and working memory that is in progress but not completely onboard may make it hard for them to remember all of their job responsibilities and the order in which they should be done. Encouraging them to make lists and take notes as they are given instructions can ensure that they will follow the directions of their employer and maintain that job. Emotion regulation and stress tolerance, to which adoptees may not have full access, can make it hard to handle constructive criticism or redirection from an employer. Remembering these things and keeping the door open so that a child can come talk to their parents about the hard things at work will mean that parents are the resource and refuge their child needs them to be. During childhood, parents were a safe place for their child. Even in young adulthood, parents can continue to hold that space. They can continue to be a safe emotional place in which their child can be vulnerable and talk about things that are hard. When adoptees can share this with parents, it allows parents to offer assistance through problem-solving or teaching new skills. This is the best way to come alongside the adoptee and help them through the hard places of young adulthood.

Another transition to consider is that when parents are no longer paying the bills for their child, the relationship may change. When the child lived at home and their parents took care of them, that was a large part of the parent–child relationship.

The child needed parents to provide for them because they could not provide for themselves. The relationship was transactional: parents paid for things that their child needed. The child got something physical and tangible from their parents.

However, when parents stop paying for things, when their child becomes financially independent and can provide for themselves, this can change the foundation of the relationship. Adoptees no longer "need" parents in a physical sense, but they still desperately "need" parents in an emotional sense. The relationship shifts from meeting physical needs to meeting emotional needs. This is the transition that every parent–child relationship goes through during the young adult years.

The difference in adoptive families is that adoptees may struggle to have an emotional relationship with parents. A physical, transactional, relationship can feel more comfortable to them. An emotional relationship requires vulnerability and sharing, which is hard for adoptees.

In a biological family where a child may have been raised trusting their parents from birth, this transition is easier because the emotional relationship has always been there. For adoptees, trust is hard-won. They struggle to trust because relationships have provided pain in the past. Parents have worked hard for the trust they have been given. Yet, the relationship may be lacking full trust. This makes it harder for the adoptee to have confidence being vulnerable with parents. When an adoptee makes a poor choice with consequences, being vulnerable with a safe person and asking for emotional support or help with problem-solving is much harder. In fact, when parents are no longer providing for adoptees' physical needs, they may even feel like they do not need parents and may walk away from the relationship. In their perception, there is no use for a relationship that is not physically sustaining because they may not find value in emotional relationships.

It is not surprising that we are talking about the relationship between the adult adoptee and their parents in the middle of the section on money management and employment, especially since it seems transactional as opposed to trust-based. This is something that the two of us have talked about often and have in common with our children. Our children see us as a source of good things, but perhaps not because of any emotional connection.

But the point is that regardless of our adult adoptees' chronological age, it is our goal as the parent to continue to reach out and build emotional connection, despite or because of the simplified, transactional, on-the-surface relationships our child is satisfied with. That isn't okay with us! We still say "yes" more than "no" because we want to. My husband and I (Elaine) look for ways to insert ourselves in their lives. We try to pay attention to the things that are important to them, even now, so we can connect. We also want our children to see how healthy adult relationships look and continue to model for them how to be an adult, what a healthy marriage/intimate partnership looks like, how to practice good communication skills, and how to apologize when needed.

As adults in relationships, the same principles apply, they just look different. Attunement is present when we meet each other's needs, such as giving a ride to work, childcare, or a listening ear at the end of the day. It's important to remember that balance needs to be present for the relationship to be healthy. If an adoptee remains dependent on their parents, needing them to take care of everything all the time, this is not balance. In the same way, parents depending on their child for everything all the time is not a balanced, healthy relationship. The balance is interdependence, where we mutually and respectfully meet each other's needs out of care for each other. This is not the way that a young child's relationship works with a parent. Children are dependent on their parents, and this is developmentally appropriate. A relationship between parents and a young adult child looks different.

However, parents also must keep in mind that with developmental delays, the child's trajectory may not be on track with what is developmentally appropriate. They may be behind and in need of more supports for longer periods of time than their peers. The challenge is that the adoptee often wants to be doing the same things their peers are doing, even if they are in different places developmentally. Sometimes, although it is hard, parents can take a step back and let the child try for something even if they are not ready. This allows them to see for themselves that they are not ready without it becoming a power struggle between parent and child. For instance, if a teen wants to work but parents know they are not ready, helping them to complete applications, taking them to interviews and getting them a uniform are things parents can do to be supportive. Hearing from the boss that they were fired because they were not ready allows parents to be the soft place where their child can land when faced with the disappointment. Adoptees may need parents' support longer than their peers, perhaps well into young adulthood, so the transition from a dependent to interdependent relationship may take longer.

Once adult children are moving along that spectrum from dependent to interdependent, parents can think about the ways they can meet their needs in attunement. The key is to think about which of the child's needs parents can meet. Resentment happens when parents meet more of their child's needs than they are comfortable doing. Think about what the adoptee needs, and then about which of those needs you can meet, offering that support with confidence so that the child can depend on it. For example, if the adult adoptee needs childcare while they work and a parent is retired, that may be a need the parent can meet. If parents have health conditions that make it difficult to run after toddler grandchildren, they may offer to watch the children two days a week or pay a portion of the childcare costs if they are able. Each parent will be able to offer different things to their child. Every situation is different. Parents can agree to drive their child to work when their car is in the shop but not every day. They can offer to bring dinner once a week (that provides a ton of leftovers) when they know their child is struggling financially. By thinking about what needs they are able to meet and then meeting them, parents can build attunement between parent and adoptee, reinforcing that the child is valuable, seen, heard, and understood.

These things build trust. As a child learns that they can depend on their parent, emotionally and in an adult relationship, they can rest in their parents' care. They can trust their parent to show up and be there because they have reliably done so. This trust deepens the relationship and parents become a safe place for the adoptee where they can share in vulnerability and find validation and support. A securely attached adult relationship is the result. Parents create a place that their young adult child can return to when life is hard. They make vulnerability safe. They offer support, understanding, validation, problem-solving, and comfort. Then adoptees can go back out into the world to try again.

Spirituality

All parents raise their children with a set of beliefs about the world around them. Every parent has their own beliefs that they model for their child, which the child then adopts or rejects. Often, as parents, our own beliefs are a result of our parents' modeling. Even parents who raise their children with no spirituality are passing on the belief that there is no spirituality. Part of being a parent is molding and shaping another person. Children watch and listen to parents' modeling, as they learn about the world around them. Those parents who want to raise a blank slate child who can make their own decisions about things like spirituality are nevertheless still creating beliefs simply by not supplying any. This is the miracle of relationships, that we "rub off" on each other. Within the connection, I learn from you, and you learn from me. Our children learn from us, and we learn from them (especially things about themselves!).

For those parents who raised their child with a belief in God or spirituality, investing in the child by giving them a religious foundation, it can be painful when they reject those beliefs. Parents invest in their child in this way because they believe this foundation will help them in life, giving them a source of peace and comfort and a relationship that will bring identity and meaning to them. It can be hard to watch adoptees choose to walk away from what parents have lovingly invested. In the same way, seeing the child reject their investment in morals and character qualities leaves parents grieving as their child walks down a different path in life.

Adoptees struggle, perhaps more often than their peers, with spirituality and a relationship with God because of their trauma. When a person experiences trauma in childhood, when they have believed that someone would save them from abuse or neglect or feeling alone and maybe even asked God to save them but continued to feel abandoned, this has an impact on their ability to believe in a loving, caring God. When they feel they have asked God for help and He has not heard them—or has even ignored them—this can become a barrier to growing a healthy relationship with God.

Helping adoptees to understand that God has a purpose in the pain, even if it remains unseen, can help to redeem the experience. Not "redeem it and make everything that happened to them okay," but redeem it to take something meant for harm and use it for good. That trauma created strengths in adoptees that would not have been there if they had not survived hard things. That trauma may have prepared them to have compassion or empathy for others that will be used in their work or relationships.

An example of this is the story of Joseph in Genesis 37–50. Joseph was betrayed by his family, specifically by his brothers who sold him into slavery. He was forced to leave his country, people, and family. He lost his identity and went to a new country where he had to adjust to a new language, culture, and life. He was forced to be a slave, was falsely accused of a sexual assault, and was placed in jail. For years he remained stuck in jail, and no one believed his innocence. Joseph, in moments where he could have been helpless and hopeless, both in Potiphar's house and in jail, instead chose to work hard. He earned the respect of Potiphar and was given control over the household before Potiphar's wife accused him falsely. He earned the respect of the jailers and was placed in charge of sections of the jail. His brothers meant to harm Joseph, but God had a bigger plan and used him to save not only the Egyptians but also the Israelites. When Joseph was raised to leadership in Egypt, it was because he interpreted Pharoah's dreams about a coming famine and had a solution. Joseph saved several people groups because God built into him the ability to rise above a struggle. Joseph was a survivor and found his strengths when faced with challenges. God took the hard parts of his life and used them to prepare Joseph to be a leader.

Another applicable story is that of Moses in Exodus. His mother lovingly placed him for adoption because she knew that she could not keep him safe or provide for him. He was raised by another mother, in another culture, in another socioeconomic status. His adoptive mother was a princess! When he went searching for his identity and discovered who he was, Moses wanted to get to know his Israelite family and spend time with them. But they rejected him, and he ran to a distant land to spend decades recovering. God did not waste those painful experiences in Moses's life. God had bigger plans, much bigger. Moses lacked confidence. He doubted his abilities. He experienced anxiety and maybe even depression. Nevertheless, God used Moses, and his learned knowledge of the Egyptian culture, to free the Israelites. God molded and shaped Moses into the leader that He meant

Moses to be. No pain was wasted; no experience unredeemed. God takes what Satan means for harm and turns it into good.

It's important for parents to recognize that as much as they invest spiritually into their child, each person has their own personal relationship with God. You cannot gift your child your faith. Parents can teach and share but as a child reaches the age of accountability, they become responsible for having their own connection to God. Children must make their own choices, and as painful as it may be to watch them walk away from all that their parents have wished for them, they have their own path to walk. They may walk away and return at some later time, especially as they are able to find meaning in their pain. When they begin to see how their trauma is being used to mold and shape them into strong adults who can understand the pain of others and reach out in empathy, their view of God may change. The anger that they may have experienced toward a God who "allowed" these things to happen may transform into thankfulness for a plan in their life. Sometimes the development of executive functioning skills like rationalizing and reasoning (some of the last skills to develop, which may be further delayed in the adoptee because of their trauma history) can help the adoptee see their journey through a different lens. They may also walk away and not return, but that is their choice.

If parents can remain who they have always been, holding onto their beliefs and spirituality, then adoptees can continue to access those things through their parents. There are times they may call and say, "Since you pray, can you pray for . . ." They know who their parents are and what they believe. When they have questions or wonder about thoughts regarding spirituality, they know that they can come to their parents. Keeping the door open, remaining nonjudgmental, and loving unconditionally will keep those lines of communication open.

Dreams Deferred and/or Lost

There are two types of lost dreams that adoptive families may need to deal with: the parents' and the child's. Adoptees had dreams about what the future would look like. Some may be realistic, others unrealistic. Some may be positive and others negative, like believing they will struggle with substances like their biological parents might have. It can be hard for adoptees to accept limitations they may have, such as those delays that mean they are not developmentally ready for what peers their chronological age are experiencing. Adoptees will have grief and loss associated with those deferred and lost dreams. It's important for parents to validate the adoptee's feelings and experiences, letting the child know they are seen, heard, and cared for. Help them to care for those feelings of loss and move through them, because those feelings are real. They are not imagined or exaggerated. They are actual losses that generate feelings of sadness and even fear that they may never achieve their goals. If left uncared for, these feelings of sadness and fear can grow to anger. Yet remember, if a child is already angry, sadness is the root.

Helping the adoptee identify their abilities, set goals, and achieve them can restore feelings of hope. When parents are supportive of their child's dreams, in whatever capacity they can reach them, this helps the adoptee to believe that they can be successful. It may mean that the child wants to get a job but is not ready for a professional career. Helping them to be realistic about what they can achieve and take steps toward the goal (perhaps by completing applications for an entry-level position) can be the support they need to feel validated and valued, providing encouragement that will motivate them to larger goals.

The other type of dreams that may have been lost or deferred are those of the parents. When parents have a child, whether biological or adopted, they dream. They hold that child in their arms and dream about what their life may look like. These dreams motivate parents to mold and shape their child. When the child shows an interest in soccer, parents may register them for a team and take them to practice, dreaming that one day they will play professionally. When they play with doctors' toys, parents may imagine them as a doctor. When parents see them reach out to their friend who is hurting, they may imagine them having a life of helping others. Parents dream. They think about who their child is and who they will be.

When a child struggles, whether with a mental illness, an intellectual or physical disability, or trauma-induced developmental delays, it can create feelings of pain and loss in parents. No matter who the child is, chances are small that the dreams parents have for their child are the ones the child will actually achieve. A child has their own life, thoughts, and choices. They have their own dreams for their life. It is the role of the parent to not live vicariously through them. Parents are not meant to fulfill their own life dreams through their child's life. Parents are meant to come alongside their child, walk beside them and support them in the pursuit of their own dreams.

The hardest part is seeing a child struggle. Adoptees often struggle more than their peers. No parent wants their child to face struggles and pain. Maybe a parent looked forward to their child's high school graduation and instead they dropped out or graduated from a residential treatment center. Perhaps a parent dreamed about teaching their child to drive but because of limitations that is not something they will be able to do.

A poignant moment for me (Christina) was when I was standing in the checkout line at a preteen clothing store and being waited on by a teenager the same age as my daughter. My daughter was developmentally delayed and still wanted to wear clothes that a younger teen would wear. In honoring this and meeting my child where she was, I was confronted with the teen working at the checkout and what I dreamed my daughter would be doing at this age but was not. It was really hard, and I choked back the tears as I checked out of the store.

It is important to recognize the feelings of grief and loss this creates in parents—and to take care of those feelings. Parents' feelings are real. They deserve expression, whether through writing, drawing, or a word spoken to a trusted ear. The loss of the dream that a child will be "okay"—because adoptees may not be "okay" for large periods of time—is painful. When parents care for their emotions and find their own emotion regulation—that "calm, cool, and collected-ness"—a child who is also struggling with the loss of their dreams can learn their emotion regulation from their parents.

Apologizing to Our Kids

One last type of hard conversation adoptive parents must sometimes have with adoptees is apologizing to them. Parents are human. There is no perfect human. Humans are fallible. Parents are fallible. Parents are not perfect. Parents make mistakes. Sometimes parents' mistakes are related to not being aware or informed. Perhaps they didn't learn about the impact of trauma on their child until they were a teenager and parented them by giving consequences for behaviors which they now know were defense mechanisms and survival skills based in fear. Perhaps they parented their child in the way they were parented instead of with a trust-based, relational lens. Perhaps they yelled and screamed when their buttons were pushed, resulting in their child being afraid of those emotions. As parents learn about parenting a child with trauma experiences—as they know better— they do better.

At these times, as parents become aware that they could have done things differently with their child, an apology can bring healing to the relationship. When there has been a rupture, a separation in a relationship, apology is the social skill that is used to heal the relationship. An apology means the following:

> a. I did something that hurt you and I acknowledge that (even if I did not do it intentionally);
> b. I'm sorry you were hurt, and;
> c. I will try hard to not hurt you in this way again.

Parents can honestly say to their child that they hurt them, that they are sorry about that hurt, and that they will try not to hurt them in this way again because they now know better. This apology can completely change a relationship, even with an adult child. It means that parents humble themselves to admit they are not perfect, they make mistakes, and they didn't "know it all" about parenting. When parents can do this, the healing it provides to the adoptee and the relationship is priceless.

In addition, how can parents expect a child to apologize to anyone else if they have not had this social skill modeled for them? When parents model apologizing, children have an easier time accepting that apology heals and repairs relationships. They are building into their child's understanding of relationships and how they work. Even when the adoptee is an adult, having hard conversations like this can facilitate further learning from their parent.

Parents and Helping Professionals Takeaway

- Our children are precious, even when their choices are not. We can separate the child from the behavior and support the child even if we cannot support the choice.
- An adult child gets to make their own choices. This is about them finding their path, so don't take it personally when their path does not run parallel to yours.
- Be their safe place, where they are told they are valuable and that it is okay to seek autonomy. Be the open door they can return to when the world is a hard place.
- Choose your battles. Do you want to be right, or do you want to have a relationship?
- Teach your child to be safe with sexuality, that they have control and consent.
- Determine your boundaries early if your child is using substances.
- Agree on boundaries with money and if or how you will continue to meet your child's needs into adulthood.
- Your child has their own relationship with God. He knows their pain and how it has impacted their ability to trust that He is good and loving. He loved them before you knew them, so trust them to His care.
- Dreams have been lost—both yours and your child's. Take the time to grieve your losses so that you can help your child to grieve theirs.
- As parents, we can apologize if we realize we have hurt our children. When a relationship has been ruptured, apology is the way to repair and reconcile.

Adult Adoptee Takeaway

- Your parents most likely want to be your safe space, comfort zone, and refuge when the world is a hard place. They want you to come to them when you need help problem-solving. There may be hard conversations, but you are loved.
- Autonomy is part of identity, and it means that you get to decide who you will be in this world.
- Remember to be safe in sexuality. You make choices with your body and have control over consent. Healthy relationships follow this equation: (Attunement/Meeting Needs + Trust) + Vulnerability) = Attachment
- Without these steps there is a greater risk of your heart being hurt.
- If you are using substances, your parents will set boundaries to keep you and themselves safe because they love you.
- When your parents are no longer providing for your physical needs, they will still be there to provide for your emotional needs, which are just as important.
- God loves you! And He has great plans for your life. He takes painful, hard things and turns them into leadership traits. What was meant to harm you, He will use to mold and shape you into greatness.
- Your parents are not perfect. They are human and they make mistakes. Try to extend grace in the same way that you would want someone to extend grace to you for your mistakes and imperfections.

CHAPTER 7

The Prodigal

It happened again this week. "Would you have time to talk?" the text said. "Of course," my heart responded. I knew instantly what the topic was, and I knew what was needed. This parent wants to talk about her prodigal.

As a follower of Jesus, I (Elaine) refer to a prodigal by referencing the parable of the prodigal son found in Luke 15:11–32. In this story, the younger son asks for his inheritance before his father's death and "squanders it on wild living." He had lots of friends as long as the money lasted, but when famine came into the land, he had no money left. He had no friends and he finally hired himself out to feed pigs.

When there is a child who purposely turns their back on what they've been taught and rebels against expectations, they are called a prodigal. They have left the faith. They have left the family. They have cut their parents off, frequently avoiding communication of any kind. Prodigals are thought of as ones who have gotten involved with drugs, alcohol, sex, crime, pornography, smoking, truancy, cussing, homosexuality, or playing in a rock band. There are sons and daughters who are prodigals who aren't adopted, but adoptees who carry that adoption trauma with them can seem especially lost.

I have had a lot of personal experience with prodigal children. One of the challenging aspects was that my faith was an anchor I needed to hang on to throughout this rough journey, and yet the faith community was often where I found the most criticism and unhelpful advice. I would like to share with you some key things that I have learned from a positive faith perspective that I have held onto for the past fifteen years.

This chapter is my story. I share it with many thanks to my children, who have been great teachers.

Model Yourself After the Father

If we are going to refer to our children as prodigals, who are we going to be? Luke 15:20 says, "But while he was still a long way off, his father saw him and was filled with compassion for him." I pray that my heart remains soft and compassionate toward my prodigal children. I pray that I don't lose heart and give up hope for them, that I will be waiting expectantly for their return. I pray that I can remain connected to them so I have space to show my commitment and concern.

The story continues: "He ran to his son, threw his arms around him and kissed him." Every time I see one of my young adult children, I greet them enthusiastically. I want them to know they are always wanted, no matter what they've done, where they've been, who they've been with, or what our last words were to each other. I'm not even sure if they notice! But I want them to know that they may always "come home" even if they can't live here.

The other piece of this is, what does my face look like when my prodigal comes back? What do you think the biblical father's face looked like? Do you think it was squinty eyed with clenched jaw, biting back scathing, sarcastic comments? Somehow "filled with compassion" and "running toward him with open arms" doesn't go with stone-faced. Check yourself. Are you warm, open, and engaging with your young adult children?

I (Christina) love this story because I feel that God gives us an example to follow when we experience a prodigal. When our child wants to walk away from us, the tendency can be to chase them and work extra hard to engage them, yet that is not the example God gave us. When the prodigal walked away from his family, his life, and everything he had been raised to value, the father did not run after him, chasing him and begging him to return home. The father gave the prodigal his inheritance and watched him walk away. This can be hard for us as parents. It was hard for me, and I cried many tears over my prodigal. Yet if my child is choosing to walk away, believing that the life she wants is better than the one she has, and I run and chase after her, this can create frustration in my child and escalate her attempts to separate from me. I explained this to my sweet girl by drawing a diagram where she was walking away and I was staying right where I was. Relationships do not work and are not healthy when one person is chasing another. When we are raising a child, we attach to them and they are dependent on us, so relationship building continues. But when they become an adult and make their own choices, we cannot and should not force them to have a relationship with us. What I communicated to my child was that I would always be there, right where I was, and when she chose to turn around and walk back toward me, she would find me there waiting for her. This is healthy relationship and how all healthy relationships work: two people moving toward each other. They don't both have to be moving at the same pace, but when my daughter turned around, I was right there waiting, just like I said I would be. The father did not need to be told that his prodigal son was approaching—he was watching, waiting, on the porch. And when he saw his son in the distance, he began to run to him. May we all be watching and waiting!

Own What's Yours to Own (Don't Own What's Not Yours to Own)

As parents of prodigals, we can get caught up by the "tough love" scenario, which can do more harm than good in our relationship with our young adult children. What has made more sense to us in parenting our challenging kids is the concept of "own what's ours to own." When you find yourself in an estranged relationship with your child, chances are good that something went wrong. We have a ready list of all the things the child did that, if she hadn't done them, we wouldn't be in this mess. But if we stop and think, we probably could come up with a few things that we could have done better. If we are brave, we could ask our child, "Is there something I can do to help?" "Is there something you need from me to make this better?" "Have I hurt you in some way that I need to make right?"

Now is the time for you to own what is yours to own. Own your part of the dysfunction, hurt, brokenness, and pain. Even if the story they're telling is only partly true, it is their reality. Stay in that moment with them and say I'm sorry. If we are working on our connecting relationship, it is not time to work on "correcting" their thinking. None of us are perfect parents, but that is not a defense to be used at this moment. Sit with them and carry the weight of your part.

I've (Elaine) needed to own my part in my children's stories. At the same time, I can't own what isn't mine to own. There are things I can't fix. I can't fix consequences of poor choices that they've made. I can't fix delusional thoughts. I can't fix when they run out of money because they've mismanaged it. Those are not things for me to own. My heart hurts and I want to jump in, but it's not mine. I can help make a budget, file a police report, accompany them to court, or sit and listen to phone calls in the middle of the night. I need to keep these two things separate and help my children to own their parts too. My parts to own are my harsh words, inappropriate actions, things I did when I knew better or later learned could have been better. These are the things I apologize for.

Love Your Prodigal Well: Practical Tips
Parenting with a View of Eternity

As a church leader and a former missionary, I was really struggling with the reputation of having prodigal children (remember to only own what's yours to own), so I wanted to know how to love my children well without adding a layer of guilt and shame onto them. I learned that I needed to reframe what was going on in our home to an eternal perspective that allowed us to let some of the little things go. So, my husband and I started having conversations like "Smoking isn't a salvation issue!" I realized that what I really want for my children more than anything in the world is for them to know Jesus Christ. This is what I pray for and until it happens, I can't expect them to be Christlike in their behavior. So, while I know the behaviors are harmful, there is no reason for those to change until their standard is raised by a belief in Jesus and wanting to please Him instead of self. I am not okay with the actions, but those are now not my deepest concern. My deepest concern is my child's heart.

Because my deepest concern is my child's heart, I do not want to be the thing that stands in the way of them knowing Him, and so we welcome them home. As they are. "Come home. We miss you. When can we see you? Do you need to do laundry? Want to come for a meal?" And we go to them. And we text. And we FaceTime. We send memes. We tell stories and laugh. And we share Jesus. We pray.

Parenting with Open Hands

Practice with me a moment. Close your eyes. Now think of all the things you would like to control or enforce about your child. As you think of each thing, clench your fists tighter and tighter.

- I wish she would stop dressing in all black.
- He must graduate from high school.
- What are we going to do if she gets pregnant?
- How can I explain to the pastor that my daughter is a lesbian?

Probably not only are your fists clenched, but your jaw and teeth are grinding together as well. Your whole body is taut with tension. And the reality is you cannot control any of that. You can only hand your child to the Lord and represent Him well.

Hebrews 12:14 says, "Make every effort to live in peace with everyone and be holy. Without holiness, no one will see the Lord." Now go through that list again, only this time loosen your hands and lift them to God, offering those things to Him. Offer your responses as well so that you remain holy in your actions and attitudes. Breathe deep with each release. Practice the discipline of open hands often.

Parenting in Pursuit
The most heartbreaking thing I witness is when a young adult says, "You don't love me. I might as well just leave!" and the parent responds with equal anger and frustration. "Well, there's the door!" Oh, my heart! All this trauma and attachment "stuff" that we've been talking about is still at play even when our children are young adults. What they really want to know is,

- Will you still love me even if . . .?
- Am I worth it?
- Am I precious just by being me?

And our answer as we look into the face of our child, created in the image of God, should be yes. Yes. Yes.

Hold onto Hope: Coming out on the Other Side
As I have shared in this chapter, these lessons were mine to learn. I didn't have a book. Sadly, thirty years ago there was very little research on adoption trauma, and I didn't understand why my sweet girl seemed to be hurting. I believe God gave me great insight about this, and modeling myself after the prodigal's father was one of the first things that made sense to me. Loving my children unconditionally, with welcoming arms as we are loved, despite their behavior, made more sense than tough love or sanctimonious comments from others about how, if she was their daughter, they would never allow such behaviors. I knew I loved this girl, loved this boy, absolutely, desperately. I would stand in the gap for her, take on fire for him, block the flaming arrows—if I could just figure out what to do.

When we finally got some therapy, I was at the top of the list of the things that were wrong. Owning what was mine to own became my next lesson. I needed to listen to and hear the pain I had caused my child, whether I agreed with it or not. While painful at first, I needed to hear her perception of what was going on. I needed to hear how decisions my husband and I made had hurt her, driven her away, pierced her heart, made her feel. None of that was our intention, but that was not the time to defend my choices.

Slowly and painfully, we have grown. Sometimes forward. Sometimes backward. I am most pleased that I have a continuing relationship with each of our children, and I believe we have an increasing level of trust and attachment even at this age.

My daughter has become more public with her story of grief, loss, and trauma. We came to the understanding that her story and my story would not be the same. We were going to be okay with that. I am so proud of her that she has become strong enough to process the things that she has gone through and can encourage others. After one particularly raw social media entry, she received feedback from a family friend who chastised her for not taking my feelings into account. This friend knew how much I loved her and was trying to reach her. My daughter quickly called me and asked, "Did I offend you with what I wrote?"

"No," was my response. "I was very proud of you and know that it's your story." She read me the response she was sending back to the family friend.

"You haven't stayed in touch with me since those days, so you don't know that my mom and I have a very strong relationship now. We have both apologized and have grown together as we worked things out."

I am grateful that my husband and I have connected relationships with all our children. And my prayer is that through us, they will glimpse the heavenly Father who loves them most of all. Prodigals do come home.

Parents and Helping Professionals Takeaway

- Look to the Father of the prodigal. He set an example that we can follow, and He knows our hurting hearts.
- Own what's yours and apologize. But don't own what's not yours—and know the difference.
- Love your child by praying for them and giving them to Jesus. You cannot control them, their choices, their life path, or their relationship with the Lord. You cannot control whether or not they want to have a relationship with you. God knows your heart, so talk to Him about it. You have a common interest: You both love that child!
- Hold onto hope. Don't lose your hope. The story is still being written. The last chapter is unknown.

Adult Adoptees Takeaway

- If you are thinking about or have walked away from your adoptive family, know that your parents still love you.
- Parents are not perfect. They make mistakes. Sometimes they do and say hurtful things. It does not mean they do not love you.
- If you said and did hurtful things too, know that *you* are not your words and choices. Your parents love *you*, even if they don't love your words or choices.
- You and your parents may not agree on a variety of topics, but it is possible to agree to disagree. Many relationships still exist because of this fabulous principle.
- Reestablishing communication can be the first step to healing the relationship. Reach out today and try sharing with your parents how you're feeling and what you need from them.

CHAPTER 8

The Unimaginable

In our work and in our lives, we have come face to face with the unimaginable: the death of an adopted child, perhaps by drug overdose or suicide. A run-in with the law that results in a lengthy jail sentence. Mental illness so severe that hopes of your child living a life as a functioning member of society seem like a far-away dream.

The hope of having a family built by adoption has been crushed and burned because someone in the relationship has said, "I'm not putting up with this anymore," and the door has been shut, never to be opened again. For the adoptive parent, the birth parent, or the adoptee, the loss is great. Done. Gone. Dead. Hopeless. Empty. How does one find healing and hope in relationship when the other side of that relationship isn't there?

I (Elaine) was in a conversation with a mother of a young adult daughter who was grieved by the recent events in her daughter's life. The daughter was making bad decisions and poor choices. Due to her limited understanding, the adult adoptee had no idea of the ramifications of the societal and legal trouble in which she was involved. All this adult child knew was that she did not want anyone else to tell her what to do.

I gently reminded the mom that while on the surface it seemed like her daughter was making these "choices" and now would need to "suffer the consequences," the reality was, her adult daughter wasn't really choosing her behavior as if it was an informed decision. Rather, she was impulsively reacting to senses, triggers—whatever her body and brain were leading her to do. There was very little thought involved in the choices the child was making.

The mother was distraught because she could see her daughter falling apart. As her legal guardian, she was struggling to brainstorm how she could help. To make matters worse, her daughter had turned against her in the worst way, with homicidal ideations. She was cutting off their connections, the ones that the mother had worked so hard to cultivate. This mother was devasted. How do we begin to repair this? Can it even be repaired if the adult child does not want to reconcile?

Another recent story was in the news regarding a young adult who had been adopted internationally from Korea. Throughout his life he had struggled with being bullied at school because he was different. He had challenging behaviors as a child due to early childhood trauma and lack of attachment. These issues were addressed as behavioral needs instead of emotional, relational, and trauma-based brokenness. He was given a list of diagnoses, but the treatments were not helpful.

The boy began using drugs and committed crimes to feed his habit. He was placed into a juvenile detention center instead of inpatient hospitalization. A hospital may have addressed his complex, deeply rooted needs instead of reinforcing the internal message of "I'm bad." At the end of the story, the young man was at a bridge, ready to commit suicide. The police talked him down, but when he turned to face them with his arms raised, it appeared that he was armed. He was shot and lost his life on that bridge. This is the unimaginable that some families experience and is the reason why understanding the involvement of trauma is so important.

A favorite part of my (Elaine) job is to train camp counselors as they prepare to work at Christian camps for the summer. In my brief trainings with them, I try to reframe campers' "bad behavior" into a look at what else could be going on. I focus on giving counselors more effective responses to deal with these situations. Inevitably I get a few counselors that have been adopted, and they often ask if they can talk to me for a moment. As they have shared their stories, I have learned that my training has handed them so many pieces that were missing from their own understanding. They want to know more. I normalize their struggles and big feelings and encourage them that they are going to make it.

I ask these camp counselors about their parents and if they can talk with them. Silence. The road has been tough sometimes; communication hasn't been good. I hand the youth my card and say that they can have their parents call me. I am more than happy to talk to them and meet with all of them together. Many times, providing education about the traumas experienced in adoption and reframing the child's choices and behaviors helps to bring healing and understanding to families.

These stories are heart-wrenching. You have your own story, and it may be painful. You may be experiencing the unimaginable. We are sorry. It can be so hard.

What can you do when you are walking in the unimaginable? Many of the tips given in this book still hold true even then. I (Christina) walked this road recently with my daughter. So many unimaginable things happened all at once that for several months it felt like the walls were closing in. I was struggling to keep my perspective and remain a connected parent. There were times when I thought about disconnecting because the pain was too great. Relationships can be painful, especially if the person you are in relationship with is struggling in a lot of big ways.

As we have written this book over the last several years, as each of us has come across a situation with one of our children, our constant refrain has become, "Is it in the book?" If not, we have added a chapter. As I walked this path, there were many calls to Elaine, who made the time to talk to me and help me make sense of the mess that life had become. She knew enough to send a message: "How are you? Should we Zoom?" She understood the unimaginable because she has been there too. As we said, "Is this in the book," we came back to these principles:

- Own what's yours to own and don't own what's not yours to own (chapter 8). What part did you have to play in where you find yourself? If you can't change the outcome, you can seek counseling and encouragement from others to process, rectify, and forgive yourself for what you did wrong and what you could have done differently. Let go of the things that are not yours to carry. Forgive yourself. Forgive your child.
- Practice good self-care (chapter 13). Keep the bar set at a manageable level for yourself, especially if you are dealing with some huge losses or catastrophic events. It's okay for life to go on without you for a little while as you are getting what you need: adequate rest, good nutrition, exercise, fresh air.
- Surround yourself with people who understand (chapter 13). This will be very important, especially if your situation is related to your adoptive relationships. There are a lot of people who make assumptions without understanding the complexity and trauma involved in adoption. They will have recommendations and critiques that are not helpful and may even be hurtful. They simply do not understand. Find the people who do understand. Other adoptive families at your church or in your community may understand. Support groups (in-person or online) can be helpful. Find your village and spend time with them, allowing them to speak wisdom and encouragement to your heart.

- Float. This strategy was not mentioned before, but we have found this to be especially helpful when you are feeling undone. Picture this: you are feeling pummeled by waves, taking on water, barely holding on, struggling to tread water, and thinking you are going under for the last time. A lifesaving skill they teach young swimmers when they are tired or can't get their breath is to roll over onto their backs and float. Float. Let the water hold you up. Rest in it instead of fighting against it. Roll with the waves as they come.

Isn't that a beautiful concept? You can apply it in this darkest of situations. You are at the end of yourself. You've tried and not given up, yet you arrive at an impasse: jail, hospital, death, closed doors. Your family is gone or changed forever. Simply float: Flip over to your back and float. Rest. Feel the buoyancy of the water holding you up. You've been fighting for a long time. Maybe it's night and the stars are twinkling overhead. Your mouth is above the water, able to take in air. Breathe. Be still.

Adult Adoptees, Parents, and Helping Professionals
Takeaways

- The unimaginable can happen in any family.
- Own what's yours to own. Don't take on the responsibilities of someone else's choices. Each person makes their own choices, and those choices may hurt us.
- Take care of your emotions—they are real! Practice self-care, then surround yourself with supportive and understanding people.
- Grieve. Do not try to fight, push away, or stuff the sad, devastating feelings. For in fighting, we exhaust ourselves but the feelings don't dissipate. Let the tears and sadness come. Learn to float and ride the waves because feelings change. They come and go, lessening and intensifying.
- If you know someone going through the unimaginable, sit with them. Consider Job's friends. Their being present and not leaving him alone in the unimaginable was what helped him. What was not helpful was when they opened their mouths to speak. Sometimes words are not needed. Bring coffee or tea and simply sit. Be present. Be still.
- Some verses on which to meditate:
  - He heals the brokenhearted and binds up their wounds. (Psalm 147:3)
  - Be merciful to me, Lord, for I am in distress; my eyes grow weak with sorrow, my soul and body with grief. (Psalm 31:9)
  - The Lord is close to the brokenhearted and saves those who are crushed in spirit. (Psalm 34:18)
  - Weeping may remain for a night, but joy comes in the morning. (Psalm 30:5)
  - My flesh and my heart may fail, but God is the strength of my heart and my portion forever. (Psalm 73:26)

- For no one is cast off by the Lord forever. Though he brings grief, he will show compassion. So great is his unfailing love. For he does not willingly bring affliction or grief to anyone. (Lamentations 3:31–33)
- But you, God, see the trouble of the afflicted; you consider their grief and take it in hand. The victims commit themselves to you; you are the helper of the fatherless. (Psalm 10:14)

CHAPTER 9

Mental Health Needs of the Adult Adoptee

The experience of trauma impacts mental health. Feelings of anxiety and depression can result from a person not feeling safe and not knowing whom to trust. Losing their biological family can cause the adult adoptee to feel sad and struggle with unresolved grief. In addition, a history of abuse and neglect can lead to dissociation as they look to create a safe place in their mind if there is no physical safety available to them. It is common for mental health symptoms to be present when a person has survived trauma, and adult adoptees are included in this demographic.

Struggling with mental health symptoms can make life feel overwhelming. It can cause a person to have difficulty managing their life. If an adult adoptee has not learned to manage their symptoms by adulthood, they will struggle even more with the transition to independence. Introducing the following tools early and helping the child learn how to use those skills effectively can make the transition to adulthood easier.

For the person who struggles with mental health challenges, learning interventions and coping skills that they can use to control and "be in charge" of the symptoms can help them find feelings of competence and confidence. Interventions and coping skills are tools that parents can give to their children. Medication is another tool; often it can help bring stability and balance both emotionally and biologically. If an adult adoptee is in treatment, keeping that treatment consistent throughout the transition to independence can be a support that contributes to their success.

Parents can support their children in many ways when it comes to their mental health, such as helping them to understand what emotion regulation is and modeling coping and calming strategies when emotions are growing large and there is a need to regain control. Everyone has different things that calm them when they are angry or scared, or that lift them when they are feeling sad. Since trauma is recorded into the brain through the five senses and is also triggered by those senses, sensory coping strategies often work best—for instance, essential oils on cotton balls, chewing bubble gum (calming), or spicy gum, like peppermint (energizing). Kinetic sand is a good tool for fidgeting and working out feelings with hands. Listening to music can soothe and quiet emotions. Movement is also a helpful coping strategy, especially when adrenaline is involved (as it is in feelings of angry or scared). Walking, exercising, or yoga can be calming when experiencing those strong emotions. Helping the adult adoptee learn to regulate, or control, their emotions is essential to social success.

Parents can encourage an adult adoptee to continue using their tools or to stay in treatment. Normalize treatment for them as a benefit and a support that helps them achieve their goals. Emphasize that stability is needed for them to be successfully independent. If the adult adoptee had mental health services as a child, continue those into adulthood. Many child services can be continued until age twenty-one. Just because a child turns eighteen does not mean that they no longer have access to child programming. Often, the way parents frame the services helps the adult adoptee agree to continue them. When parents frame the services as supports that contribute to their child's stability, emphasizing that stability leads to independence, the child feels that their parents are partnering with them to reach their goals—because they are! Whether the adult adoptee's goal is to live in their own apartment one day or to have their own family, when parents partner with them to find ways to reach their goals, they understand that they can trust their family as safe people who care about them.

It is important to know what services the adoptee qualifies for in childhood, as these are often linked to adult services that become available as the child ages. Learning what services are available can be as simple as asking the child's therapist or psychiatrist; they are often aware of services and can refer to them. If a child is not in mental health treatment, parents can talk to the child's school guidance counselor or social worker, or check with the state or county mental health authority. This is normally a government agency that provides case management to individuals with mental illnesses, including children.

The public school system where we (Elaine) live has excellent special education services. When it came time to prepare for transitioning my son to adult services, they were very supportive. He was allowed to continue with his emotional support classes and job skill training up until age twenty-one through the school district. They worked with us on developing a transition plan and walked beside us to get adult services set up so there wasn't a gap in services. It normalized the continuation of services for my son and has now been a part of his life for ten years. Even if your school district has a less than stellar program, they are responsible to give educational assistance to the students in their district.

Case management is valuable as well—even life-sustaining. A case manager is an individual assigned to the adult adoptee to make sure that they receive any services they qualify for. This is important because someone with mental illness often does better with wraparound programming. For instance, if they are diagnosed with major depression and struggle with lack of motivation, low mood, and low confidence, then a supportive employment agency (described below) would be a helpful service and one they most likely qualify for. A case manager would know about this service, could complete the application, and secure the support. Having a case manager means the adult adoptee does not have to research and find the services themselves. Each service listed below has different criteria for eligibility; a case manager can help navigate this. Case management can follow the adoptee into adulthood.

Another mental health service the adult adoptee may qualify for is employment assistance programming (referenced in the previous paragraph). This agency provides career testing to help someone determine what their strengths are and in what types of jobs they would function well. They can arrange paid or unpaid internships in those jobs, allowing the adult adoptee to try them and see if they like them. They can attend training programs and even college classes, often paid for by the agency. They offer job coaching in the form of a person who will go to work with the adult adoptee at the beginning and help them adjust and assimilate to the work environment. The job coach can also help them learn how to communicate and negotiate with their employer.

There are also day programs that support individuals struggling with mental health, in which they can learn coping skills and interventions. If the adult adoptee is having difficulty managing their symptoms enough to hold employment, this is an option that can help them learn to change what they can control and cope with what they cannot change. This program can act as a transition into employment: The adult adoptee can work to find a job, then attend the program on days when they are not working.

Also available are mental health-based adult group homes where the adult adoptee can take steps toward independence while still having support and supervision to help them. A group home is a place where four to eight people live together with twenty-four-hour staffing to help with cooking, driving them to medical appointments, administering medication, and encouraging the use of new thinking and new behaviors learned through therapy. This is a way to help adult adoptees spread their wings and have the independence they want while giving parents the peace of mind that their children are not alone. Many of these programs also have step-down affiliates that allow them to rent a floor of apartments in a complex so that each person lives independently in their own apartment. The apartment at the end of the hall is a staff office where the individuals can go if they need help, to problem-solve, or just to talk about something. The goal is for the adult adoptee to have their own apartment eventually, but to get there by taking baby steps. In this way they are not overwhelmed by independence, which can be overwhelming even for the young adult who does not struggle with mental illness.

Another housing support is Section 8, which provides a rental supplement to allow a person with mental illness to be able to afford to live independently when they do not make enough from working to provide for themselves. This reduces their rent to an affordable amount. There are certain housing complexes and landlords who accept Section 8 payments. This can also be a service that the adult adoptee outgrows when they begin making a living wage.

Adult adoptees may also qualify for Social Security Disability Income, which can be a large support. Individuals with serious mental illness that impacts their ability to work and earn a living wage can qualify for a monthly payment that allows them to provide for themselves. This can pay for housing, food, and transportation, helping them take steps toward independence. If they move from part- to full-time employment, they can gradually outgrow this entitlement as well. If they do not outgrow it, it will remain available to them if their symptoms impact their ability to hold employment.

It is important to know crisis support services as well. If the adult adoptee is ever in a mental health crisis, they may need supports outside the family. Search for the local suicide hotline, mental health crisis hotline, and the police non-emergency numbers. Crisis support can sometimes respond in place of police when someone is having a mental health crisis. They can help to de-escalate and, if needed, can complete an emergency petition for an evaluation at the hospital. They can also help the individual get connected with a therapist and psychiatrist for ongoing treatment. If a parent ever thinks they might need to call and request law enforcement support—for instance, if the child ever becomes a danger to self or others—it may be beneficial to have a conversation with the local law enforcement office beforehand. Introducing the family to the officers, having the child see police in a non-threatening way, and allowing the officers to see the child while not escalated can help everyone frame an incident later on by better understanding the people involved. Having a list that can be handed to the officers in advance and/or when they respond to a call containing some helpful hints for de-escalating the child may help their efforts to be successful.

It is also important for parents to find support for themselves. NAMI (National Alliance on Mental Illness) often has local support groups for family members, and especially parents, of those struggling with mental illness. In order to be supportive of the adult adoptee in the ways that will help them, parents need to take care of themselves to prevent burning out. Caring for a loved one with a mental illness by providing constant support and supervision can be hard and overwhelming work. If the parent were to burn out, the child would only have larger struggles than the ones they are already facing. If needed, parents should find a therapist who can be supportive of them.

I (Christina) walked this road with my own child. Between Elaine and myself, we have used all these supports. My daughter wanted independence, developmentally appropriate, but she was not yet ready for it. So, we compromised with an adult group home. My daughter has the support and supervision she needs and the independence she wants. And I have peace knowing that my daughter is safe. As my child learns the skills needed for independence, like cooking and money management, she is moving closer to a step-down transition into an apartment.

We created a village to help us raise our children. We knew we could not do it alone. We both knew that if we used only our own resources, our children would not have had the best opportunity for success. We cannot be with them 24/7, and it wouldn't have been healthy for us to have done that even if our schedules allowed. It was healthy for our children to see many people surrounding them with support. It was helpful for our kids to have someone other than us telling them how to achieve their goals. As mothers still in the process of building a trust-based relationship with our children, our telling them how to be successful was not something they always readily accepted. So, we found others, our villages, to speak truth and encouragement into their lives so that our voices were not the only ones they heard. This has been a positive experience for us and, while others may have their own individual experiences, this has helped our families to be able to focus on family relationships. Our village is life sustaining, both for our kids and for us. It means we do not have to be the therapist, psychiatrist, job coach, and rule enforcer—the village does those things. We only have to be the parent. And that is the role that only we can fill. It does not confuse our children, and we are still working with everyone on the "team." We still know everything that is happening, but we do not have to have our hands on every working piece. We trust the people who are supporting our kids, which helps our kids to trust them too.

Adult Adoptee, Parents, and Helping Professionals Takeaway

- When we experience trauma, it leaves us with large feelings that can be overwhelming and result in mental health diagnosis.
- Parents or mental health professionals can help the adult adoptee to learn coping and calming skills for those large and frequent emotions.
- Mental health treatment (therapy or medication) can help the adult adoptee to achieve their goals.

Supports = Stability = Successful Independence

- If supports (school and community programming) are in place during the teenage years, keep those supports in place until age twenty-one.
- Case management can help you find and secure services that the adult adoptee qualifies for.
- Employment assistance programs can provide career and skill testing, training, help finding a job, and job coaching.
- Day programs are available to provide support for the adult adoptee who is not able to work due to mental health symptoms. These programs focus on increasing stability and the use of strategies for good mental health.
- There are a variety of supportive housing options, including group homes, independent living apartments, and Section 8 vouchers. They provide the supports an adult adoptee needs to take the next step toward independence.
- Social Security Disability Income can be helpful if the adult adoptee is not making a living wage but wants to become more independent.
- Know your local crisis support providers and how to contact them in a mental health emergency.

- NAMI provides support groups for family members and parents so that they can feel supported too.

CHAPTER 10

Intellectual Disability

When parents adopt a child, they are like any other parent who is expecting a biological child. They have hopes and dreams about their child's future and about how their family will function. They think about college and careers and who their child will be, and even allow their minds to drift to weddings and grandchildren.

When that parent recognizes that their child is not achieving developmental milestones or is struggling to understand the world around them, this can be difficult to accept. Children who have experienced trauma often face developmental delays and can be far behind their peers cognitively, emotionally, and socially. Often, parents expect these delays and recognize them immediately (depending on the age of the child when they come home). Yet when years have passed and these delays continue to persist, with the child either not making any progress forward or making only small progress, parents may pursue testing in order to receive support services.

Testing may involve a psychological assessment or evaluation. This may last a day or two and involve questionnaires completed by parents and teachers. This helps the psychologist to have a better understanding of the child's skills and abilities. They will look at mental health symptoms and diagnoses as well as assess academic progress to diagnose learning disabilities. There will most likely be an IQ test and other brain function exams to assist the psychologist in evaluating for intellectual disabilities.

Upon receiving a diagnosis of an intellectual disability, adoptive parents, like any parent, experience the loss of dreams and face the need to modify expectations. Adoptees may still achieve college, career, marriage, and grandchildren, but the path may look a little different than what the parent had hoped for. Parents want good things for their child and want the best for them. The loss parents feel is not only for themselves but for their child. It hurts a parent's heart as they recognize in advance that their child's life will be filled with challenges, that they may have to work harder than others to achieve similar goals, and that they may be confronted with prejudices or discrimination.

Parents need to allow themselves time to mourn the losses and accept the reality of their child's needs. This way, parents will be operating from a position of strength and can be a support to their children in their challenges. Parents can identify their child's strengths and help them learn how to use those strengths to compensate for their challenges. Modeling this strategy can help the child see their potential. As parents identify supports that can aid the adoptee in achieving their full potential (and then normalize those supports), they can help the child to accept help. If parents can have a positive attitude about the differences in their child, then they can set the tone for how the child will view their own limitations. Adoptees will look to parents for emotion regulation and to get a sense of their personal value. If parents can be emotionally consistent and reinforce the child's preciousness, the child will most likely follow that lead. But this can only happen if parents take the time to mourn the losses and intentionally reassess their expectations.

Long before my (Christina) daughter made me a mother, I had a back surgery that left me with some permanent physical limitations. At the time, I was unsure of the purpose of my limitations, but I knew that God always has a plan. When my daughter was diagnosed with her intellectual disability, it was hard for her to grasp. I had framed it as things that she would need some help with, but someone at the school labeled it a "disability" and this upset my daughter. She struggled to accept that she would need help with certain things. I was able to relate and talk to her about how hard it is for me to ask for and accept help with my own physical limitations. She talked about the losses of the things she would not be able to do, and again I was able to relate, telling her about how I managed by focusing on the things that I could do. It is a different kind of disability, but I am now thankful for my limitations because they allowed me to understand and relate to my daughter in a way that was real and genuine, that helped her to not feel alone in her feelings.

By looking closely at the child, watching and learning them, parents can recognize where they are developmentally. They may have some tasks they can accomplish on a higher level while other, lower-level tasks may be frustrating for them. This is a result of different areas of the brain being impacted by disability. If the disability resulted from in utero drug exposure, then the child may have difficulty with tasks specific to the parts of the brain that were forming when the substances were used by their biological parent. Intellectual disabilities can also be diagnosed when a child has experienced trauma and has been spending most of their time in their survival brain, which neglects the development of executive functioning skills. In this case, targeting those areas with specific exercises can improve functioning. If an intellectual disability is present as a result of a traumatic brain injury following physical abuse, then there may not be an opportunity for progress. Providing the child with support services can help them realize their potential as a functional adult. When parents recognize where their child is intellectually, cognitively, socially, and emotionally, and meet them there, the child feels seen, heard, and understood. When parents' expectations of the adoptee match what they are capable of giving, the child feel successful and appreciated.

I (Christina) experienced this when my daughter was diagnosed with an intellectual disability. I had anticipated that she may have developmental delays after being in institutional care for most of her life and had lowered my expectations to what I thought would be a good level. However, my daughter was functioning on an even lower level than I had expected. Once we got testing results and a more accurate developmental age, I readjusted my expectations, lowering them again, and my daughter flourished. Where I used to have a girl frustrated and melting down when she was unable to meet my goals, I now had a girl meeting the goals every day and feeling happy and proud of her accomplishments. It meant that I had a sticker chart on my refrigerator door for my teenager, but she loved putting her stickers on every night!

As parents adjust their dreams and modify what they expect from their child, the child often responds in a positive way. When parents are holding kids to expectations that they cannot meet, even to age-appropriate norms, they struggle to meet them, which lowers their self-esteem and mood. When a child feels that they cannot "make parents happy" and are always "letting parents down," this can lead the child to feel sad, disappointed, frustrated, or irritable. When parents lower the bar, adjust expectations, and see their child for who they really are, the door is opened for them to succeed.

Continuing to demand age-appropriate behaviors and tasks from a child when they are unable to meet those expectations can damage the parent–child relationship. A child can feel that parents do not understand them or are being harsh. This can happen unintentionally if parents are not in tune with their child and getting to know them as they are, not as the parent wants them to be. Parents can only validate their child and their abilities when they have appropriate expectations of them. Once the child can fulfill these newly modified expectations and sees the pride and acceptance in their parent's eyes, they also find their pride and preciousness. This improves the relationship with the child as they see the light in their parent's eyes.

A variety of programs and support services can help the adult adoptee, depending on their intellectual disability. Many mental health agencies also have intellectual disability services, including after-school programs for children who need help with social skills training. If the child has a diagnosed intellectual disability, they most likely also had an Individualized Education Plan (IEP) in school that gave them accommodations and support. An IEP can continue in an educational environment until age twenty-one. Just because the child turns eighteen or finishes the twelfth grade does not mean that they no longer qualify for educational support. Often there are employment training programs or life skills classes that the child can take through the school system that will continue to prepare them to be successful and learn to accommodate their limitations.

An IEP may also open the door for community-based employment training programs in adulthood. These programs can provide support with assessing career skills and finding career options that would focus on the child's strengths. They can provide employment training through programs that teach skills or pay for community college classes that will prepare the adult adoptee for a career. This child could also benefit from a job coach or a supervised and supportive job environment.

The adult adoptee may also be eligible for social security disability, and this may help to supplement any employment income they have. They may be working in a supportive environment but without making enough money to be self-supporting. The supplemental income may make it possible for them to pursue independence. Seeking independence may look different for adult adoptees, and they may have a different path to what many others take for granted. It is important to help them set goals that are important to them; then they will be motivated to achieve them. If they want to work, help them to explore their strengths and what types of jobs those strengths support. If they want to live on their own, explore their options and make sure they understand the path to their goal.

Housing is available in a variety of forms based on the needs and abilities of the child. These housing supports are most often accessed through the county's mental health department. There are adult group homes for those who need increased supervision and support. This can afford the adult adoptee the ability to pursue independence through baby steps. These smaller increments will set them up for success by allowing them to learn independent living skills slowly and with a higher likelihood of success. Once they have learned about cooking, cleaning, public transportation, scheduling appointments, and money management, they may be ready for a less intensive housing environment.

An independent living program rents a floor of apartments so each person has their own space, with the apartment at the end of the hallway acting as a staff apartment that is staffed twenty-four hours a day, allowing the resident to seek help with cooking, transportation, medication management, or other questions when they arise. From here, a person can move to their own apartment outside the program and have intensive case management several days a week to make sure they are eating, getting to work or appointments, and being safe. These case management hours can decrease as the person is consistently successful in their independence. The person can then transition to living in their own independent apartment. If at any point the person begins to struggle with the level of independence they have, they can move back a step or stay where they are without the pressure of moving forward. Meeting a person where they are and helping them to feel confidence in their strengths improves their mental health, too.

Some parents prefer to keep their child at home with them as opposed to pursuing residential programs, however, it is important to allow the child to make choices and decisions if they voice a desire to pursue independence. There may be concerns about how others will meet the child's needs as opposed to how the parent(s) meet them. Indeed, it is likely that the parent knows the child better than anyone else and meets their needs consistently and effectively. However, it is also important to consider the adult adoptee's thoughts, feelings, and desires. Often, a solution is for parents to offer choices, such as making progress toward independence by living with them or moving to an adult group home. In both instances, they will learn steps toward independence. The child can truly make progress in either place, and if they are allowed to make the choice, they will feel empowered and respected. Having a conversation with the child about this and talking about the decision together can improve the relationship, ensuring that they feel heard and understood.

As parents age, it is important to consider long-term planning for the child. Once parents pass away (since the child will most likely outlive the parent), what will happen to the child? If there is family that can step in and continue to provide the care that the parents now provide, then there is a loving arrangement. However, if parents do not have that type of family support, then it is also loving to plan for the child and think about what they will need.

Along with assessing the child's needs and abilities in order to provide appropriate supports, it is important to assess their ability to be safe. When the adult adoptee has simpler processing skills or more concrete thinking, they may have difficulty with higher level executive functioning. They may struggle to problem-solve, consider pros and cons, or grasp the possible consequences of decisions they have made. This can make them vulnerable to manipulation or being taken advantage of. They may need a provision for safety. If the child trusts others too easily or has a hard time telling safe from unsafe people, they may need additional supervision and supports to stay safe.

I (Christina) once heard about a family that had a child diagnosed with Down syndrome. When their child started to talk about wanting to move out, they found a way to help her pursue her goals using an adult group home, supportive employment, and a social security disability supplement. The parents said they wanted to transition their child to her next living environment while they were still able to help her adjust. They wanted to be there to take her out for lunch and help her form relationships with others at her new living environment. They said they did not want her to be overwhelmed when they passed away by losing her parents, home, and way of life all at one time and without their support in the transition. This was a loving decision to do what was best for their child, to ensure that her routine and supports would be in place and well developed when she lost her parents and needed supports the most.

Another dynamic to assess as a child approaches the age of eighteen is if you think the child may need a legal guardian. Parents may also be able to answer that question by asking these questions:

- Can the child understand and make decisions about their health and medical needs?
- Can the child understand the legal implications of situations or make decisions about legal matters?
- Can the child understand money and handle their own finances?
- Is the child able to keep themselves safe, recognizing dangerous people who may try to take advantage of them?

If parents answered "No" to any of those questions, their child may need a legal guardian. The purpose of a legal guardian is to make those decisions just reviewed. The process varies from state to state but it will most likely follow these steps:

1. Write a letter to the local court that handles guardianship cases, often the Orphans' Court. Outline the concerns about the child's ability to keep themselves safe and make these decisions. Include a psychological evaluation diagnosing the child's intellectual disability and any recommendations that came from that evaluation. Also include their IEP as further supportive documentation. List out any supports or programming that they are currently receiving.

2. A court date will be set, and an attorney will be assigned to the child. The attorney representing the child will be one who is volunteering to act as the child's attorney, pro bono. They will come out to meet with the parent and then the child, explaining to the child what is happening and discerning if there is an argument the child wants to make in their favor toward not having a guardian. Parents can retain their own attorney at their own cost if they would find it helpful to have someone explain the process to them and represent their concerns.

3. The psychologist who diagnosed the intellectual disability will need to testify in court to their findings and recommendations, including whether the child is competent to make medical, financial, and legal decisions.

4. The judge will decide if the child needs a guardian and if so, will seek to identify that guardian. If their parent is willing to serve as the guardian, then this is what the court would consider first. If a family member is not able or willing to serve as guardian, then another independent guardian will be assigned. In these cases, it is a qualified individual who agrees to serve as a guardian for several people who need one. The guardian is called any time a medical decision

needs to be made, including changing medications or approving medical procedures. They are consulted in legal matters and manage the person's money, including becoming the representative payee for the social security disability payment and paying the individual's bills.

There are several things for parents to consider when deciding whether to be the adult adoptee's legal guardian. There are positives to becoming their guardian, including the parents' love of their child and desire for what is best for them. Parents will be more responsive to their child's needs and wants than a third party. If the child calls asking money because they want to join the gym down the street, parents are more likely to run it over that day or the next. A non-family member who is appointed guardian for the child may respond that the child can wait until the checks go out at the beginning of the month. Helping a child understand that they need assistance and support can be framed by explaining that a stranger can help them or their parents can, but that parents would love to continue to help them after the age of eighteen because that is what family does. Coming alongside and assuring them that you are not leaving them alone with tasks that can feel overwhelming, and anxiety-producing (like money matters and medical decisions) can calm them.

However, there are negatives too, and it is important to balance both. A biological child who trusts their parent may readily accept their help in the role of guardian. However, for the adult adoptee who does not have a trust-based relationship with their parents, they may not like having their parent assigned as guardian. The adult adoptee may perceive that their parents have "control" over them because they manage their money and make their important decisions. They may feel that parents are treating them "like a child." It can build a wall between parents and adult adoptees, impacting the attachment work of trying to maintain a connection. Developing attachment and relationship is something most adoptive families struggle with continuing well into adulthood. Being a child's guardian can complicate this.

I (Christina) had this experience. I became my adult child's legal guardian because I love my child and wanted to be the one to protect her and help her. However, in my child's search for independence and her desire to pull away from parents in the transition to adulthood, my sweet girl struggled to accept my help and support. Instead, the guardianship placed a block between us, and our relationship did not improve over time. This was most likely impacted by me adopting my daughter when she was a teenager, so our relationship had not had adequate time to grow and deepen. Not all may have the same experience. I decided to rescind my guardianship, returning it to the court and asking them to assign another guardian. In this way, a separate individual would handle my child's important decisions and I would be free to reengage in relationship building with my daughter.

I (Elaine) had a similar experience with one of my children. My husband and I did not seek guardianship, allowing our son to be "his own boss" even though he struggles to hold down regular employment and lacks financial understanding. We had a good enough relationship at the beginning and remained involved, so we felt like things could be managed. This son made friends with a negative influence who persuaded him that we were trying to control him, undermining years of relationship building. This "friend" convinced our son that he did not need to be on his medication, and his psychosis became worse. It was a very challenging time. We called Adult Protective Services several times just to put violent incidents on the record. Thankfully, the community supports stayed involved as another voice of reason, and even though we weren't permitted to speak to the supports, since we were no longer legal guardians and he was "of age," they understood the parental role we have with our son as part of the team that cares for him. The "happy" ending was that this negative influence went to jail, and slowly our son realized his mistakes and has returned to some better choices.

When a child has been diagnosed with an intellectual disability, another consideration is end-of-life planning. When thinking about what parents want to leave their children, it is important to consider what the children can manage. If the adult adoptee has difficulty managing money and has a legal guardian, then leaving them a gift of money may be complicated. Speaking to an attorney who specializes in special needs legal matters can help parents to design a will or establish a trust with the state laws in mind. Some states allow a special needs trust that will make funds available to the child that they can use for things that social security disability does not cover. These will be funds that cannot be taken or impact the child's continued receipt of their entitlements and community supports. Having access to a large amount of money can disqualify someone from medical assistance or social security disability, making them responsible to pay for their current community-based services. This would use up their inheritance quickly, and they would then have to reapply for services and entitlements that might no longer be available to them. Instead, a special needs trust would allow the sum of money to be available to the child for the rest of their lifetime, only for certain items that are not covered by entitlements. A trust will require a trustee who can administer the funds, but this is easily arranged with relatives or a bank.

There are so many things to consider when a child has been diagnosed with an intellectual disability. They will need supports in childhood, and often the need for those supports can continue into adulthood. Not ending those services and supports when the child turns eighteen is important. Look to the adult system to provide similar supports through case management and community-based agencies, as this can allow someone to successfully transition to adulthood and everything that this will mean for them. It will look different for each child, as their capabilities and skills will vary, but using their strengths to achieve their potential will create in them a sense of pride and the confidence that they can set goals and achieve them. If the child wants to work, find a way to partner with them to realize their goals. Supportive work or volunteer opportunities may fulfill their desires. If the child wants to live independently, then look for programs that will provide the support and supervision they need while also affording parents the peace of mind to release them to independence. Take time to consider if the adult adoptee may need a provision of safety and the additional supports provided by guardianship. Carefully decide as the parent if you want to be the guardian, if one is needed, or if the court should be asked to assign someone. Being the parent of an adult child who has continued needs for supervision and support can be challenging, so parents need to make sure that self-care is a priority. Breaks are needed in order to remain refreshed and ready to be the parent on whom the adult adoptee can depend.

Adult Adoptee, Parents, and Helping Professionals Takeaway

- If you feel developmental delays are present, schedule a neuropsychological evaluation with a psychologist.
- It is important for each person to mourn lost dreams in order to adjust expectations.
- Meet the adult adoptee where they are. Assess developmental age as opposed to chronological age and provide supports in that space.
- Under the child's IEP, pursue vocational, social, and life skills training before a) they leave school or b) their IEP ends at age twenty-one.
- Employment training programs can help prepare and support the adult adoptee at work.
- Social Security Disability Income can help if a living wage is not being earned. Some adult adoptees, depending on ability, may volunteer instead of work, and this income makes it possible to pursue a meaningful work goal.
- There are housing supports like group homes, independent living programs, and step-down programs where a person lives in their own apartment and has a case manager come to the apartment for several hours a week for support.
- Assess safety and the need for a guardian. Consider whether parents would be the guardian or if the judge would be asked to assign one.
- Speak to an attorney who specializes in special needs trusts to make sure your child will be provided for after you have passed.

CHAPTER 11

Physical Disability

When adopted children have physical disabilities, there is another layer to the process of growing up. As if being adopted is not enough, the child must also (with the help of their adoptive parent) navigate through the maze of physical challenges. One of my (Elaine) daughters has right hemiplegic cerebral palsy. She has a great sense of humor and can find the ridiculousness in people's outspoken responses to her asking if her leg is broken or unabashedly asking what is wrong with her. But her recent launching to college has been hard, and some things have not been funny.

First, finding a college with reasonable accommodations was harder than it should have been. During her college tours, able-bodied people were not considerate, nor did they seem to be cognizant of how many staircases existed on the campus. Elevators tended to be hidden in dark corners—if the student guide even knew where they were in the first place. Bullying still exists on college campuses; instead of compassion, my daughter was told that she "clumps when she walks."

Because it requires a lot of physical stamina to get from one building to the next, she took her adult trike to campus for transportation. She puts her books in the basket and can ride from her dorm to class. Her trike has been stolen as a "joke." Even with the trike, her pace is still different than other students'. She recently said that the biggest factor in making friends at college has been others' willingness to slow down to keep pace with her. However, she can list many kind acts as well, like people helping her with her tray and silverware in the cafeteria when she could not manage walking and carrying them at the same time. One young man walked beside her as she rode her trike, waited as she got off, and carried her books into the dorm. There is another girl who just watches out for her, notices her, makes sure she is not left out.

In preparing for this launching, we were mindful to use high school as practice, where she could learn to advocate for herself. I didn't completely remove myself from the picture, but as situations arose, I would ask my daughter is she wanted me to step in or if she wanted to handle it. We would discuss which situations felt like they needed to be addressed and which ones should be let go. We didn't always agree on this, so it was good to be able to examine it together. We would discuss who the best person to talk to might be—the person with whom she had the issue, or a person with authority? We would work through the talking points, determining which things were important and needed to be addressed, and which things could be let go because bringing them into the conversation could be harmful or hurtful. And of course, we discussed how she was feeling about each situation (which was probably the easiest with her, since she is the child with the best emotional processing skills). Ultimately, the hope is that the adoptive parent's behavior modeling will teach the adopted child to accept themselves and to not see their physical disability as a flaw or something that holds them back. My daughter said that when the parents model acceptance, openness, and a willingness to talk about the issues the child faces, the child has permission to learn about themselves and how they want to be part of the world.

I (Christina) have worked with parents who have walked this path with their children. We always brainstorm ways in which the child may need some extra support, then problem-solve how to provide it. The important part is partnering with your child to ensure you provide what they need you to provide and no more. This increases their self-confidence and self-esteem. I love how Elaine said that she and her daughter discussed what needed to be done to address things and then determined if her daughter wanted to address the issue herself or wanted Elaine's help to do so. This empowers a child to advocate for themselves while reinforcing that they have support and are not alone. It has been a joy to watch Elaine's daughter find success in college as she grows and develops into a successful young woman. These stories give us hope and encouragement as we work with other families.

Adult Adoptee, Parents, and Helping Professionals Takeaway

- Brainstorm how the adult adoptee's limitations or needs will impact them as they transition to the adult world (e.g., elevators at college or places of employment, etc.).
- Teach your child about the Americans with Disabilities Act, their rights, and how to advocate for themselves.
- Offer assistance but keep the lines of communication open so your child can tell you what they need help with.
- Assist, but do not do too much. Listen to the adult adoptee, and as they use their voice, praise their confidence. Adult adoptees need to be empowered to autonomy. Parents can be the cheerleaders, letting the adult adoptee know they are not alone.

CHAPTER 12

The Importance of Self-Care

Every book about parenting and adoption has a section about practicing self-care. It is hoped that by this point in the journey the importance of self-care is understood, but it is still so difficult to achieve. There is a look that an over-extended mother gives when she is told, "You need to practice better self-care." The eyes heat up as they prepare to assail the advice-giver with a deadly swarm of flaming arrows for mentioning a concept that is so elusive yet bantered about so glibly. Sometimes the look freezes while the mother mumbles something between gritted teeth, like, "You can talk to me about that once you've walked in my shoes." Other times the fire is doused by a torrent of tears as the mother covers her face with her hands and sobs. It is hard to receive the message of self-care while feeling misunderstood about the level of pain one is carrying.

At a particularly complex and challenging time, I (Elaine) had finally convinced one of my children to go to a counselor. It was my first real foray into navigating mental health support for my children; I was just thankful I got her in the car and to the appointment. Once the therapist got her into his office, he "empowered" her by sharing with her that since she was over the age of fourteen, she did not need my consent to be there, she didn't need to agree to treatment, and I couldn't make her go. This was music to her ears! She waltzed out to the waiting room and announced, "He said I didn't have to stay." I then proceeded to melt into a puddle of tears on the floor.

It was then that I resolved that our situation needed help—and if she wasn't going to get any, then I was. I saw that counselor for a year. In hindsight, I probably should have found someone else (he wasn't that great), but I did not have the energy. I cannot think of anything he brought out in me or helped uncover, but it was my one space where I could talk without having to watch my words or think about how they would impact someone else. He was outside my circle, and sitting with him allowed me the opportunity to hold things up and examine them a little more objectively. It allowed me to name my own feelings. We often talked through situations I had faced and the alternate responses I might have given—responses that might have worked better and resulted in different outcomes.

This chapter will be based on self-care solutions that have worked in our personal and professional circles, based on insights, mistakes, conversations, and support groups.

Operate from a Position of Strength

During their teen years, I (Elaine) started to understand that to truly help my children, I needed to parent them from a position of strength. What that means to me is that I am bringing my whole, my best, my healthy and secure, my "as full of well-being as I can be" self to the table. This takes the pressure off my children to be responsible for my emotions. They have enough to be responsible for on their own.

Grieve the Losses and Recognize the Pain

Since I want to operate from a position of strength and take care of my emotions, I must grieve the losses and recognize the pain. For example, I verbalize, albeit not very loudly, that I hate

Mother's Day. I just do. I don't think it's because of my infertility, but my whole motherhood journey has been really, really hard and I don't think Hallmark has a card for it. My husband and I have had to give up our dream of living overseas as missionaries. We just won't be able to leave our children, even though they are of adult age, for that long of a time. The funny thing about grief is that we don't always know when a wave of it is going to hit. As we've helped our children navigate the grief and loss of their adoption traumas, we've seen this hold true for them. But it is also true for us. I can be driving down the road on my way to work when a thought hits me and my heart hurts like shards of glass in a burlap sack in the middle of my chest. I am so sad for all the losses that the members of my family have experienced, and I start to weep.

Nurture Your Faith

My first and main self-care principle has been to nurture my faith in Jesus Christ and align myself with a biblical worldview. Understanding creation, the fall, redemption, hope, forgiveness, purpose, and a promised future gave structure, framework, and meaning to the chaos of the life I was living. Believing in someone bigger than myself—someone with a broader view of the beginning who was orchestrating other parts of the story—helped me keep my role in perspective. It meant that I didn't have to have all the answers. I could throw myself back into the greatest trust fall of all time. I cultivated my daily conversation with the Lord, crying out to Him but also listening. I spent time reading His Word so that His voice would be familiar enough for me to pick it out of the daily cacophony. Don't misunderstand, I was not highly disciplined with regular times of prayer and devotions. It was often snatches-of-breath prayers, like, "Dear God, I need you!" or, "Reveal yourself," or, "Give me your strength," or simply feeling the sun on my face as His warm embrace. Additional ways of spiritual self-care are staying connected with a body of believers, spending time in musical worship, and being fed spiritually by someone who is more spiritually mature, whether through books, podcasts, discipleship, or mentorship.

Create Space for Yourself

As I think about parenting from a position of strength and taking care of myself spiritually, I am also aware that I need space for me. To be attuned with me. I have a mental image of running my hands over my arms and legs, checking for any broken bones and bruises. "You okay, honey?" I say to myself. I fix a cup of coffee and have a moment. "How are you?" I ask myself. I give myself time to name my feelings and tell myself that those feelings are valid for me to have. And then, with the second cup of coffee, I remind myself that feelings aren't truth. It's good for me to have time to process all of that. I'm really quite reasonable!

Find Your Own Supports/Friends

Another important part of self-care is making sure you have supports for yourself. Whether that means therapeutic sessions with a counselor or a weekly massage, take stock of the meaningful relationships in your life. Doug and I (Elaine) are partners for life, and we have worked through some pretty tough seasons. I am so grateful that he is a huge part of my support network. My husband and I have decided that it's really hard to have good friends at our age, especially when you've had as curious and "exotic" of a life as we have. While we can laugh at that, I still, even after all these years, get a little envious and cynical at the generational family photos at the beach with everyone wearing khaki shorts with white polos. We can hardly vacation together because the needs and sensitivies of our family members cannot tolerate that level of togetherness!

"One size fits all" friendships are hard to find. We have different friends to meet different needs. We have friends of different generations. We've become the "older, wiser friends" of "younger, fun friends" who are up for game or movie nights. We have same-age friends who like to sit around with coffee to discuss theology and the meaning of life. We have friends from across the globe with whom we have journeyed for a time, who have known us in another context—these friendships feel golden, purified in fire.

Having friendships as adults can help us return to feeling and acting like grown-ups. When our children were little, we quickly felt like our brains turned to oatmeal and we couldn't put a thought together. But when children enter young adulthood, a different thing happens. We can't seem to jump-start our brains into having independent, adult thoughts. Of course, as we've been discussing, we can't leave parenting behind completely. But it is good to allow ourselves to redevelop that part of our identity.

Find Activities You Like
Cultivating regular activities with our adultg children individually and together is important. Cultivating activities without children is equally important! We've taken up some new activities with our emptier nest: kayaking on a local creek, rescuing two huskies who need extra discipline, landscaping, and gardening. Instead of driving around to tournaments, recitals, or sessions, we have had time to develop new hobbies or skills that keep us active and interesting. Read books that don't have anything to do with your life (I'm fond of British murder mysteries!). Be still, be present, and pay attention to your thoughts, feelings, sounds, smells, senses. Take time for a mini vacation or a day trip. It's your turn.

Find People Who Like to Take Care of You
When you are in a caretaker role, it is important to let others take care of you. Be ready to say yes and offer some tangible ways friends can help. Things like meals, transportation and returning books to the library are all helpful. I've also gotten pretty good

at advocating for myself and giving myself permission to say no. I don't need to be in charge of neighborhood crimewatch and church potluck and the visiting sisters of benevolence! I give you permission too!

Once when I was under considerable stress, had been ill, and was suffering from depression, a counselor told me that as helpers, we often act like a canal. The water channels through us from its source to its destination but leaves very little impact on its way. The ground is still hard, the grass is still dry. Instead, it is better to be a reservoir. As we sustain, we are also sustained. As we hold water, life around us is abundant. I like that picture of self-care. I like the thought of being a reservoir, of being sustained so I can sustain others.

In this season of parenting our young adult adoptees, we are finding many things that bring us joy and hope! We are enjoying our emptier nest. We love being grandparents. We are having fun being owners of huskies. We find ourselves having more opportunities to speak into the lives of colleagues and friends who are younger than us and encourage them in their marriages and parenting journeys. My husband and I find that we not only love each other, but *like* each other, even after thirty-five years! We find other ways to stay connected to Africa and have done short trips that fill our hearts. We want to be healthy in all ways so that we can bring our best selves to the ones we love and care for. Caring for yourself is not glib advice, but truly a sound way to live.

My (Christina) mood is always my best indicator of my self-care status. When I feel myself getting grumpy or irritable, when I feel my mood dipping or my energy level falling—it's time for self-care. Those are my indicators, my "check engine lights." What I have learned over the years is to not just be reactive in my self-care. Sure, I can wait until my check engine light is on to engage in self-care, but I can also be proactive. I can practice self-care daily so that I have fewer times when I feel low, irritable, or grumpy. I can take care of my feelings (because this life creates big feelings in us) when they are small instead of ignoring them and letting them grow larger. I can take good care of me so that when my child needs me to be the consistently calm, unconditionally loving mama I want to be, I am ready!

<u>Adult Adoptee, Parents, and Helping Professionals Takeaway</u>

Self-care is important for everyone.
- Practice it daily.
- Be proactive in self-care, not just reactive.

Operate from a position of strength and fulfillment.
- Is your love tank full, half full, or running on empty?
- Make space for the pain and grieve the losses.

Nurture your faith and lean into it on the hard days.
- Jesus asks us to give Him our burdens.
- You can trust Him—He can carry them so much better than we can.

Create space for yourself and the things that are important to you.
- Make time for yourself, even if it is twenty minutes a day to drink coffee on the porch.

Find your supporting friends, people that you have fun with—and then spend time with them.
- Find things that calm you and do them regularly. Knitting, running, kayaking, karaoke . . . you choose!
- Find people who like to take care of you. You work hard and are worth being taken care of! Find the caretakers and allow them to bless you with the gift they have been given.

Conclusion

As we close, more than anything, remember that parenting never ends. It is a journey we are on with our children. There will be mountaintop days where goals are achieved and celebrations are had. There will be valley days when tears flow and losses are grieved. There will be many days of hard climbing, where we can't see the goal and it feels like we are on our hands and knees trying to reach the next plateau.

This journey is not our own. This is the journey of our child. We are merely companions on the trail. The adult adoptee, whose life started with trauma, has a long road to healing and health. When we adopted this child, we promised to be with them on that road. We said, "You are no longer alone in this journey. We are here." Their journey does not end at eighteen. It carries on. And because we promised they would not be alone, we carry on too. Maybe it's harder than we thought it would be. That's fair. This life is probably harder than your child thought it would be, too. Knowing they don't have to face it alone—that they don't have to do this hard life on their own—lightens the weight they carry.

This is the blessing that family provides. That we are not alone. God places us in families. He gave Eve to Adam because it was not good for him to be alone. He places children with parents because it is not good for them to be alone. The family provides nurture, care, teamwork, and togetherness. The health of a family has been shown to be the largest factor in a child's ability to be resilient after trauma. Family relationships have a healing quality. They provide a safe place where we are accepted and can be vulnerable. Where we can talk about the hard things, finding comfort and refuge. This is what we provide to our children, no matter their age.

There is a greater family: the family of Christ, where we care for each other and encourage one another. There is accountability and there is love. We are told to not give up fellowshipping because God knows how much we need it—another person to share our joys and pains with; people to walk beside on this journey called life. We break bread together and share meals. There is a sense of belonging and acceptance. Jesus turned no one away. The prostitute was welcomed in. The tax collector who was a thief was welcomed in. The leper whom no one else wanted to be near was welcomed in. All sinners, all welcomed. You, me, and our children are welcomed in. Does our family reflect the family of Christ? Family is important. It is the foundation our children need when their world is crumbling or crashing and burning. Are we welcoming them in?

When working with parents of adopted children, we often see them getting stuck in the mire of behaviors. Elaine encourages them to look up and out, to "parent toward eternity." What she means by that is to focus on gaining a perspective of what is important. Is it being kind or wearing clean socks? Is it perseverance or eating green beans? The same holds true for parenting the adult child. We parent them with eternity in mind, asking, "What's important?" We want to continue modeling the kind of person we want them to be, not getting stuck on things that are irritating, frustrating, or disappointing. We have a choice and a responsibility to guide them without losing our own emotion regulation. We can practice good self-care in order to be the consistently cool, calm, and collected parent they need us to be. We can take care of our emotions so they do not interfere in our ability to continue building a relationship with our child.

As we have examined the role of trauma on brain development and specific topics that might come up for your adult child, we hope you have felt encouraged. We hope you can understand the "why" of your child's behaviors and realize that it still has little to do with you. Our children's challenges are not a personal attack on us. They are struggling, and as they struggle, we struggle with them. Because we love them. You can continue to be that safe place to land, to process, to share. When you feel overwhelmed by your adult children's unhealthy decisions and think things will always be this way, remind yourself that *now is not forever*. Just because it feels this way now, doesn't mean it will stay this way.

As you travel this road, know you are not alone. We are here with you. There are many of us on this road. We are all navigating the same twists and turns, valleys, and mountaintops. We mourn with you as you grieve the valleys and rejoice with you on the mountaintops. We walk beside you. You are not alone.

When our children walk in the door, unless it is unsafe, our response will be warm and welcoming, without comment on cleanliness, smell, appearance, or length of time apart. This is unconditional love—loving positives and negatives, on good days and bad, forever and always. They are greeted warmly with open arms. I am their forever mom.

Biographies

D r. Christina Reese has been working with children impacted by trauma and their families for the last twenty years in Baltimore, Maryland. Dr. Reese has worked with adoptive families and with children in foster care, focusing on attachment.

She has been the Director of a Mental Health Clinic and for eight years she was the case manager of a Cold Weather Shelter, working with homeless individuals and families. She is a licensed clinical professional counselor in Maine, Maryland, and Pennsylvania, and is a licensed clinical supervisor. She received her PhD in Counselor Education from George Washington University in Washington, DC. Dr. Reese's research includes the study "A Qualitative Study of Gang  Desistance in Former Gang Members." She travels internationally with PESI, a continuing education provider, training mental health professionals in creating Trauma-Informed Schools, working with Mental Health in the Classroom and Attachment and Trauma in Children. She is a TBRI practitioner and owns Felicity Counseling Services in Pennsylvania. Dr. Reese has authored the books Attachment: 60 Trauma-Informed Assessment and Treatment Interventions Across the Lifespan, Puzzle Pieces, The Attachment Connection, Trauma and Attachment and The Socially Confident Teen. She is the adoptive mother of a now young adult with special needs.

Elaine Shenk has worked with Bethany Christian Services of Central Pennsylvania since 2010 and is currently serving as the satellite office director of the Harrisburg and York offices.

She is the adoption supervisor for Domestic Adoption and

provides oversight to Post Adoption/Post Permanency Services, which help adoptive parents to seek and acquire the community supports they and their children need while providing encouragement, resourcing, and support groups for these families. She oversees the Safe Families for Children Program, which is a preventative program designed to keep kids out of foster care by providing a support network to the parents while hosting the children. While relatively new to the child welfare field professionally speaking, Elaine and her husband have been adoptive parents of four children, all now adults, for thirty years, and she has worked hard to continue to give her adult children what they need for continued attachment and development. Elaine is passionate about helping others have healthy relationships where wholeness and healing can happen.

Printed in the United States
by Baker & Taylor Publisher Services